Effective Christian Ministry

EFFECTIVE CHRISTIAN MINISTRY

Dr. Ronald W. Leigh

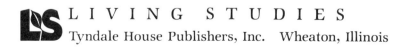
LIVING STUDIES
Tyndale House Publishers, Inc. Wheaton, Illinois

With gratitude to my teachers,
Drs. Harold Garner, Gene Getz,
Mary LeBar, Lois LeBar,
Larry Richards, and Norma Thompson

Scripture quotations are from The Holy Bible,
New International Version; Copyright © 1978 by
New York International Bible Society

First printing, September 1984
Library of Congress Catalog Card Number 84-50712
ISBN 0-8423-0733-8
Copyright © 1984 by Ronald W. Leigh
Printed in the United States of America

CONTENTS

PREFACE

If you are alive, you are affecting others. Your actions and words are determining in part what others around you think and do. You are affecting others even when you are silent or are absent from them, because others will think or act differently than they would had you been there. As long as you are alive, others' lives are different *because of you*. Your influence may be positive or negative, but it will always be there. *If you are alive, you are changing the lives of others.*

So the question is not, Shall I influence others? That question is already answered for you; you *are* influencing others. *You are a minister, an educator, a counselor!* The real question is, Am I having a positive and effective influence on others?

Obviously, as Christians we sincerely want our influence on others to be positive. Unfortunately, even though influence is involuntary, positive and effective influence is not automatic. Many times Christians say and do things which they hope will be helpful to others, but their words and deeds are a hindrance rather than a help. Often this happens because they are not making use of the basic principles of Christian influence.

The following pages attempt to explain some of these principles, which are based both on the Bible and on valid findings from such fields as psychology, sociology, communication, and education. The principles apply equally to such areas of Christian ministry as Christian education, counseling, parenting, pastoral ministry, and missions.

ONE
FOUNDATIONS
OF CHRISTIAN
MINISTRY

PRINCIPLE 1
The Bible and the Holy Spirit

PRINCIPLE 2
The Goal: Salvation and Christian Maturity

PRINCIPLE 3
The Process: Spiritual Growth

PRINCIPLE 4
The Christian Worker's Character and Attitudes

THE BIBLE
AND THE HOLY SPIRIT

 PRINCIPLE 1: True Christian ministry always involves the Bible's teachings and the Holy Spirit's activity.

There are all kinds of ministries that are not Christian ministries. They include the personal and spontaneous ministries that parents perform for their children, the huge governmental and international agencies that work with millions of people every day, and everything in between. But only a small percentage of all ministries are truly Christian. What sets a Christian ministry apart from all others?

THE BIBLE AND THE HOLY SPIRIT

A true Christian ministry always involves the Bible and the Holy Spirit. The Bible (properly interpreted) and its teachings (properly systematized) supply the main message and content of all Christian ministry, whether it is preaching, teaching, counseling, publishing, or broadcasting. If anyone ignores the Bible in his ministry, his ministry is not Christian. Likewise, the Holy Spirit supplies the spiritual dynamic of all Christian ministry. When the Holy Spirit is not active there can be no spiritual results from the ministry. There may be psychological results, but no spiritual results.

Christian ministry is aimed at two basic kinds of results, salvation and spiritual growth. Scripture makes it quite clear that *both* the teachings of the Bible and the activity of the Holy Spirit are involved in *both* salvation and spiritual growth.

	Salvation	**Spiritual Growth**
Bible	*The Bible's teachings are involved in salvation.* "The holy Scriptures . . . are able to make you wise for salvation" (2 Tim. 3:15). "Faith comes from hearing the message" (Rom. 10:17).	*The Bible's teachings are involved in spiritual growth.* "Scripture . . . is useful for teaching, rebuking, correcting and training in righteousness, so that the man of God may be thoroughly equipped for every good work" (2 Tim. 3:16, 17). "Asking God to fill you with the knowledge of his will . . . in order that you may live a life worthy of the Lord . . . growing in the knowledge of God" (Col. 1:9, 10).
Holy Spirit	*The Holy Spirit is active in salvation.* "He [the Holy Spirit] will convict the world of guilt in regard to sin and righteousness and judgment" (John 16:8). "Unless a man is born of water and the Spirit, he cannot enter the kingdom of God" (John 3:5).	*The Holy Spirit is active in spiritual growth.* "We . . . are being transformed into his likeness with ever-increasing glory, which comes from the Lord, who is the Spirit" (2 Cor. 3:18). "The fruit of the Spirit is love, joy, peace, patience, kindness, goodness, faithfulness, gentleness and self-control" (Gal. 5:22, 23).

PSYCHOLOGICAL FACTORS TOO

An individual's psychological experiences are often mistaken for the activity of the Holy Spirit. There is an important difference between the supernatural work of the Holy Spirit and a person's natural psychological functions. On the one hand, we need to understand this difference. But on the other hand, we must not oversimplify this difference by saying that when the Holy Spirit is at work, the person's normal psychological functions are not, or vice versa.

Suppose a young man publicly dedicates his life to the Lord. One observer might say, "The Holy Spirit was certainly at work." But another observer might say, "No, that young man just got worked up emotionally." Perhaps both of these observations are oversimplifying a complex event. Of course, strong emotional feelings and reactions can be falsely labeled as the work of the Holy Spirit. However, often both the Holy Spirit and strong emotions are at work at the same time.

When we claim that the Holy Spirit must be at work for a ministry to be a Christian ministry, we are not saying that other factors are not also at work. Indeed, a wide variety of psychological factors are involved in every Christian ministry. Personal motives, fears, social pressures, emotional reactions, need for recognition, fatigue, disposition, conditioning, false guilt, identification, rationalization, and competitiveness are only a few of the many psychological factors that can enter into any ministry. But nothing spiritual is happening in a ministry unless the Holy Spirit is involved *in addition* to these psychological factors.

Furthermore, the Lord often works indirectly as well as directly. For example, he worked indirectly when he made use of such natural things as locusts and wind (Exodus 10:13; 14:21). So we should not be surprised if he makes use of people and psychological factors as well. The question is not simply, Are these results caused by psychological factors or by the Holy Spirit? Rather, the question is, Are these results caused *merely* by psychological factors, or is the Holy Spirit also at work?

In any Christian ministry, psychological and spiritual factors are often present side by side. It is helpful, in carrying out a truly spiritual ministry, to be able to distinguish between these two. If we cannot detect psychological factors at work, we may mistakenly identify human manipulation as the "conviction" of the Holy Spirit. Or we may mistake some of our own fears and motives as the "voice" of the Holy Spirit. Or we may observe mere group dynamics and emotional experiences and call it the "moving" of the Holy Spirit. It is wrong to explain all religious activity as psychological. But if we label everything that looks like religious activity as from the Holy Spirit, we are just as wrong.

This subject of psychological factors and how they relate to the work of the Holy Spirit is a matter that should be discussed more fully. Several other principles, including Principles 5, 6, and 7, will describe some of the inner dynamics of the individual, and under Principle 16 we will discuss psychological conversions.

NECESSITY OF RESPONSE

We have emphasized the necessity of the Bible and the Holy Spirit. But this does not mean that every ministry in which they are involved will bring about positive results. Suppose that we clearly and prayerfully present the gospel message to a friend, with the leading and the power of the Holy Spirit. Does that guarantee that our friend will accept Christ? No. That is *his* choice to make. Or, suppose that a pastor faithfully and prayerfully teaches his congregation that they should be honest in filling out their income tax forms, and he teaches this under the leading and power of the Holy Spirit. Does that guarantee that each person in his congregation will actually be honest? No. Each person makes that choice for himself.

When we are ministering to another person, whether or not a positive result comes from our ministry *depends on the other person,* even though our ministry involves the teachings of the Bible and the work of the Holy Spirit. The other person's response makes the difference. *He* must decide to make the positive response of faith and obedience.

Some may feel that the above idea casts a poor reflection on the power of the Bible and the Holy Spirit. They may argue, based on such passages as Hebrews 4:12 and Isaiah 55:11, that any presentation of God's Word (especially any presentation blessed by the power of the Holy Spirit) must produce a positive result. But that is certainly a false interpretation for two reasons. First, the correct interpretation of the above passages must take their contexts into account. Note that earlier, in Hebrews 4:2, the writer claimed that the ancient Israelites had a divine message preached to them, "but the message they heard was of no value to them, because those who heard it did not combine it with faith." This verse clearly indicates that the response of faith is a necessary ingredient in bringing about a positive result. The context of Isaiah 55:11 indicates that the phrase "my word" refers not to the Bible as a whole, but to God's specific promise to preserve the nation Israel. Second, other passages must be taken into account. For example, consider Jesus' parable of the four different kinds of soils in Matthew 13, Mark 4, and Luke 8. In each of the four cases the Word was sown, but in each of the four cases there was a different result, not caused by a different message, but by a different inner condition in the person who heard the message. Also, we should consider the many times when Jesus ministered both to his disciples and to strangers. Sometimes those listeners failed to learn their lessons. Some of them rejected Jesus and what he taught. Some of them repeatedly lacked faith. Was this because Jesus failed in some way? Did he neglect scriptural truths and values in his teachings? Did he attempt to minister merely on a human level, with no divine power? Certainly these cannot be the proper explanations of these failures. In every case, when an individual responded negatively to Jesus' ministry, he made that choice for himself.

Thus, we can say that the Bible is *necessary* for a spiritual productive ministry, but it is not *sufficient*. This does not degrade the value of the Bible, but is a recognition of the importance of the individual's response. We can also say that the Holy Spirit is *necessary* for a spiritually productive ministry, but he does not force salvation or spiritual growth on anyone. Men and women decide for themselves whether or not they will be saved and whether or not they will grow in their Christian lives.

THE GOAL: SALVATION AND CHRISTIAN MATURITY

 PRINCIPLE 2: **The goal of any Christian ministry is twofold: first, to help others become saved, and second, to help them grow toward complete Christian maturity.**

BEYOND SALVATION

The decision to accept Jesus Christ as Savior, in itself, is the most important single decision a human being can make. Salvation brings spiritual life. It establishes the believer's new relationship with God both for the remainder of his life on earth and for eternity. The relationship with God established by that decision is the basis for all subsequent Christian living and growing. In other words, the position (salvation) is basic to the practice (the Christian walk). Because of the extreme importance of the salvation decision, some Christian workers have concluded that almost all of their efforts should be aimed at getting people saved. However, this is not the emphasis of the New Testament.

The New Testament states clearly that each individual believer is to go beyond salvation and aim for complete Christian maturity. Paul preached, admonished, and taught with the goal of presenting everyone "perfect in Christ" (Col. 1:28). He also said that believers in the body of Christ are to build each other up "until we all . . . become mature, attaining to the whole measure of the fullness of Christ" (Eph. 4:13). Paul was not satisfied to stop with salvation. Rather, he worked toward the goal of guiding every individual toward complete Christlikeness. At one point Paul even expressed more concern for building up Christians than he did for preaching the gospel to nonbelievers. Even when there were still many localities to be reached with the gospel, Paul said to Barnabas, "Let us go back and visit the brothers in all the towns where we preached the word of the Lord and see how they are doing" (Acts 15:36).

Thus we have a twofold goal. Salvation is basic, for without spiritual life spiritual growth is impossible. Even though the new believer's position is perfect in Christ, his daily practice is not. His understanding of the teachings of the Bible must grow. His consistency in applying those teachings must increase. He must learn to share his new life with others. In short, he needs to grow more and more mature, more and more like Christ.

The great commission, Christ's command to his followers at the end of his earthly ministry, also encompassed this twofold goal. It is a command to contact those who do not yet know Christ (the "nations") and to teach them to obey everything Christ commanded his disciples. "All authority in heaven and on earth has been given to me. Therefore, go and make disciples of all nations, baptizing them in the name of the Father and of the Son and of the Holy Spirit, and teaching them to obey everything I have commanded

you. And surely I will be with you always, to the very
end of the age" (Matthew 28:18-20).

Since salvation is so important, Principles 8—16 are
devoted to the gospel and evangelism.

WHAT IS COMPLETE CHRISTIAN MATURITY?

The word "mature" is commonly used in two different
ways. Sometimes it is used in an ultimate sense,
sometimes in a current sense. Maturity in the ultimate
sense would refer to an individual only when he has
"arrived" at the final destination. Maturity in the
current sense would refer to any individual who is "on
schedule" right now, implying that there is a fixed
sequence or schedule which each person must follow.
Since there is this relatively fixed sequence of physical
and linguistic development in the child, it is possible to
speak of a one-year-old as mature because he can walk,
a two-year-old as mature because he can talk in simple
sentences, and a six-year-old as mature because he can
read. (Of course, neither the one-, two-, or six-year-old is
mature in the ultimate sense.) But since there is no fixed
sequence or set schedule for spiritual development, it is
better to use the word "mature" in the ultimate sense
when talking about spiritual growth. We will refer to
that ultimate destination of spiritual growth as "complete
Christian maturity."

No one ever reaches complete Christian maturity in
this life. Complete Christian maturity is spiritual
perfection, and no one is able to maintain sinlessness in
this life (1 John 1:8-10). But even though the ultimate
goal is out of reach in this life, subgoals are within
reach, and growth toward those subgoals is to be the
Christian's daily occupation.

Below are five general descriptions of complete
Christian maturity. All five refer to the same thing, yet
each one states the idea in a different way.

Complete Christian Maturity Is:
1. Being like the Father, *holy* (1 Pet. 1:15).
2. Being like the Son, Jesus, *complete and mature* (Eph. 4:13; Col. 1:28; James 1:4; 1 John 2:6).
3. Being thoroughly *adjusted to the Holy Spirit's influence* (Gal. 5:16).
4. Being consistently *obedient* to God's Word (James 1:22).
5. *Not* being selfish, proud, or independent (Phil. 2:3-8).

In one word, complete Christian maturity is *Christlikeness.*

A LIST OF CHARACTERISTICS

All of the above descriptions of complete Christian maturity are generalizations. In order actually to visualize Christlikeness, and to apply the concept to our lives, we need a much more specific description. Thus, seventy-three characteristics of Christlikeness are listed below, organized in eleven categories. Of course, this list, which is based on the New Testament commands, is only a partial list.

1. In relation to God:
–assurance of salvation
–deep love toward God
–submission to the Lordship of Jesus Christ in all aspects of life
–yielded to the Holy Spirit
–recognition of own sinful tendencies and shortcomings
–seeks to be like Christ
–sincere worship of God
–continual earnest prayer and thankfulness
–immediate confession of sins

2. In relation to the Bible:
–conviction that the Bible is God's Word
–rich knowledge of the Bible
–rich knowledge of Bible doctrine
–aware of false doctrine
–aware of religions and cults
–desire to know more about God and his Word
–able to feed himself from the Bible
–regular Bible study
–applies the Bible to his daily life (obedient)

3. In relation to evil, Satan, worldly influences:
−sensitive to sin; recognizes evil
−hates sin and Satan and desires to live apart from sin, Satan, and
  worldly affairs
−resists temptation; abstains from all forms of evil

4. In relation to himself:
−wholesome thought life
−takes good care of his body (fit, neat, clean)
−honest acceptance of himself
−humility
−joy
−peace
−self-control; self-discipline

5. In relation to all other Christians:
−unity of Spirit
−love
−understanding and empathy
−humility
−gratefulness
−patience
−forgiveness
−kindness
−not envious
−no evil speaking against brethren; no grumbling
−prays for the brethren
−is himself (does not put on a spiritual front)
−honest
−a good example
−respects the "weaker brother"
−does not falsely judge the "stronger brother"
−faithful in gathering with other Christians
−unselfish; shares
−bears others' burdens
−restores those overtaken in sin

6. In relation to service:
−knows his own spiritual gift(s)
−faithful in using his gift(s) for service
−spirit empowered; fruitful
−does all to the Lord's glory
−good steward of his time and ability

7. In relation to non-Christians:
−love and burden for the lost (such as his neighbors, fellow workers,
  school friends)

–consistent witness to the lost in life and word
–personal involvement in missions
–not slothful in business
–owes no man anything except love

8. In relation to his family:
–if child or youth: obeys parents
–if husband: loves and cares for wife
–if wife: loves and submits to husband
–if parent: raises children to fear and obey the Lord

9. In relation to the events of life:
–faces life realistically
–faces a crisis spiritually minded
–proper perspective (not "here and now," but God's will and the end
  result)
–rejoices in suffering
–not regularly discouraged nor anxious

10. In relation to civil affairs:
–cooperates in civil affairs
–subject to government and civil laws
–prays for civil leaders

11. In relation to things:
–does not love things (in themselves)
–proper use of things (moderation)
–a good steward of his money

We can use this list as a checklist to discover the areas of our lives that need improvement. Of course, all Christians need to grow in all areas, but the purpose of such a checklist would be to find the few areas that are most urgent. Growth is most likely to occur when we focus our attention on one area at a time.

The same process can be used when we are helping another Christian grow. Since all ministry is aimed at meeting needs, we must have a clear idea of the above goal, or standard, in order to identify a person's needs. Then, by concentrating on his most urgent need we can help him grow in that area.

Obviously, if the other person is not a Christian he

needs to accept Christ. If he is already a Christian he needs to strive to become more like Christ in every area of his life. As his discipler, teacher, pastor, or friend we can help him become aware of his needs and encourage his growth in one area after another. Even though the Christian's ultimate goal is to become like Christ, there are a few things about Christ which the Christian should not try to imitate. For example, since Jesus was divine, he had authority to forgive sins, but we don't. Also, Jesus remained single, but this does not mean that celibacy is for all Christians. Jesus taught that either state, married or single, can be good—depending on God's gifts and leading in the individual's life.

THE PROCESS: SPIRITUAL GROWTH

 PRINCIPLE 3: Spiritual growth toward Christlikeness is gradual and multifaceted, and requires obedience.

How does a Christian become mature? Does it happen instantaneously? Does it depend on the Holy Spirit or on the believer? What must the believer do? Or is the secret that he must do nothing?

Unfortunately there are a number of misconceptions about what spiritual growth really is. We will discuss three misconceptions and then describe the true nature of spiritual growth.

FIRST MISCONCEPTION:
CHRISTIAN MATURITY COMES INSTANTANEOUSLY

Many people mistakenly believe that complete spiritual maturity can be theirs instantaneously. Some believe it will be theirs if God so chooses. In other words, they believe that God sanctifies whom he will. Those who get sanctified can rejoice; those who have not yet gotten sanctified can only hope. Then there are others who believe that maturity will be theirs instantaneously if they follow the secret formula. In other words, they believe that there is a surefire way to become instantly mature in perhaps one or three or seven steps.

However, there are three problems with the view that spiritual maturity can come instantly. First, it implies that complete Christian maturity, or perfection, can be reached in this life. But John wrote that if we claim to be sinless, we deceive ourselves and slander God (1 John 1:8, 10). If anyone would be able to attain perfection, we expect it would have been Paul. But even Paul said he had not attained perfection; he was still pressing forward (Phil. 3:12-16. The word "mature" is used in its current sense in v. 15). Second, such a view sets up divisions among Christians, the "haves" and the "have nots." Whenever the church has divided believers into those who have the knowledge and those who don't, or those who have the Spirit and those who don't, or those who have the gifts and those who don't, or those who have perfection and those who don't, it has become disunited and a poor testimony for the Lord. Third, this view gives the person who thinks he is mature the false impression that he has no room for improvement. Such a view misrepresents Scripture, harms the testimony of the church, and actually hinders spiritual growth.

SECOND MISCONCEPTION: CHRISTIAN MATURITY COMES AUTOMATICALLY

Some believe that as we do nothing to obtain salvation, so we need do nothing to grow spiritually. They feel that growth is based on God's grace and nothing else, so it is automatic. But such a view misrepresents salvation. Certainly it is true that we do not get saved by piling up a long record of good works. But this does not mean that we don't do anything when we get saved. We do make a decision to trust in Jesus Christ, though this decision to trust in Christ should not be considered a "good work." Actually, it is just the opposite. It is an admission that we are guilty and can do nothing to merit salvation, so we must call upon the Lord for mercy and trust Jesus' death on our behalf. Thus, salvation does not come to us automatically without a decision on our part.

The view that Christian maturity comes automatically also neglects the scriptural teaching that, even though we are not saved *by* good works, we are saved *for* good works. Paul wrote, "we are . . . created in Christ Jesus to do good works, which God prepared in advance for us to do" (Eph. 2:10). Of course, these good works are not credited to us as though we performed them in our own wisdom and strength. We must rely on the Holy Spirit for power, and we must give him the credit and glory. Nevertheless, we are the ones who do the good works. (Thus, the saying which is popular in some circles, "let go and let God," can be quite misleading.) The Christian is not to be passive, as though growth toward maturity will come automatically with the passage of time.

THIRD MISCONCEPTION:
GROWTH TOWARD CHRISTIAN MATURITY
IS LINEAR

Many Christians hold the idea that Christian growth can be likened to a ladder or an ascending line on a graph. They feel that each individual believer can be placed on a certain rung of the ladder or plotted at a certain point along the line. This view does hold that growth is gradual rather than instantaneous, and requires the believer to be active rather than passive (and thus avoids the errors of the first two views). However, it has the serious drawback of encouraging comparisons and the ranking of believers. Some end up on rung four, others on rung three, etc. Such attempts at ranking can actually hinder spiritual growth, since we tend to be jealous of those who are "above" us and to look down on those who are "below" us.

While it is true that each of us will follow a path in our Christian walk, it is not true that the path, or the sequence of steps along the path, is the same for everyone. The understandings, attitudes, skills, and action patterns that are learned throughout the Christian life are not learned in the same order by all Christians. Furthermore, each attitude or skill is not a once-learned-and-done matter. Rather, each new lesson is a matter of degree, and some lessons take decades to learn. All this makes it impossible to rank one Christian ahead of another as far as his overall Christian life is concerned.

SPIRITUAL GROWTH IS GRADUAL AND MULTIFACETED

The Bible teaches that spiritual growth progresses in a gradual manner. Even the use of the growth analogy implies a gradual progression. While the positional aspects of salvation change immediately and completely, the practical aspects change by degrees. Many New Testament references point to gradual growth toward Christian maturity:

"We . . . are being transformed into his likeness with ever-increasing glory" (2 Cor. 3:18).

"We instructed you how to live in order to please God. . . . Now we ask you . . . to do this more and more" (1 Thess. 4:1, 10).

"Your faith is growing more and more, and the love everyone of you has for each other is increasing" (2 Thess. 1:3).

"If you possess these qualities in increasing measure,

they will keep you from being ineffective and unproductive in your knowledge of our Lord Jesus Christ" (2 Pet. 1:8).

"Like newborn babies, crave pure spiritual milk, so that by it you may grow up in your salvation" (1 Pet. 2:2).

Of course, this does not mean that sudden growth in certain areas is impossible. We often hear a new Christian tell how some area of his life changed suddenly when he was saved. Perhaps his use of alcohol or drugs stopped suddenly. Or perhaps his foul language changed overnight. Such sudden changes are always welcomed, but it must not be thought that complete maturity can always come in the same manner.

Also, this emphasis on gradual growth must not be thought of as an excuse for unnecessarily slow growth. No doubt, all of us should grow faster than we do; but even when we do grow quickly, we still have a long way to go.

The Bible also teaches that spiritual growth is multifaceted. The Christian life is made up of many different but interrelated aspects. Paul talks about growing up "in all things" (Eph. 4:15). At various points in his letters he gives us long lists of different sins, some of which might be conquered while others are not yet conquered, as was the case with the Colossians (Col. 3:5-8). Indeed, the multifaceted nature of spiritual growth is even seen in the fact that there are so many commands given to believers in the New Testament (some of which are mentioned in the list of characteristics of Christian maturity in the previous chapter). Growth can take place in any one of these areas at any time. The diagram on page 30 is an attempt to illustrate just a few of the many aspects of spiritual growth.

Notice on the diagram that, even though the salvation

experience itself takes place at a point in time, it is
preceded by a process and followed by a process.
Evangelism and understanding the gospel are processes
which require time. The individual must come to
understand certain things about God, about himself, and
about Jesus. This alone takes time, but if the individual
starts with certain misconceptions because of his culture
or his family background, it may well take much
longer to clear away these misconceptions in order to
make the gospel message clear. Thus, there is a process
which precedes salvation. This is not to say that
salvation itself is a process, or that one is educated into
the Kingdom of God. The pre-salvation education
process is not the same as salvation, for it merely brings
the individual to the point where he can make an
intelligent decision. If he decides to receive Christ, he is
saved instantly.

Following salvation there is also a process, but not
every aspect of the Christian life grows at once. Growth
requires us to focus our attention on one area at a time
and to make the proper decisions in that area. Of
course, it is necessary to keep the overall goal of
Christlikeness in mind, but it is also wise to focus our
attention and our efforts on one area at a time. If we
can consistently take one small step after another, first
in one area and then in a different area, we will
experience healthy growth. God often selects the
priorities for us, sending experiences our way that call
for growth in one area. We should always be sensitive
to such leading.

If we try to find an easy way to learn everything at
once, we may become discouraged. The Christian
should set his sights on specific and realistic
improvements in one area at a time. And the Christian
worker should realize that his task is not to attempt to
grow big mushrooms overnight, but to build solid lives,
brick by brick.

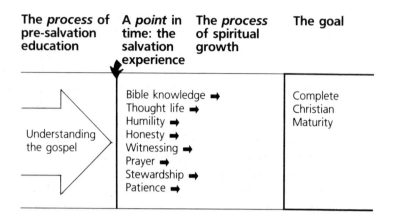

The *process* of pre-salvation education	A *point* in time: the salvation experience	The *process* of spiritual growth	The goal
Understanding the gospel		Bible knowledge ➡ Thought life ➡ Humility ➡ Honesty ➡ Witnessing ➡ Prayer ➡ Stewardship ➡ Patience ➡	Complete Christian Maturity

THE PLACE OF DEDICATION AND SPIRITUALITY

Paul urged the Roman believers to dedicate themselves to the Lord, that is, to offer themselves as "living sacrifices" (Rom. 12:1). Also, he told the Ephesian believers to "be filled with the Spirit" (Eph. 5:18). Unfortunately, some people confuse dedication and spirituality with spiritual growth.

Some feel that once they dedicate themselves to the Lord, they have done all they need to do. After all, if we are totally dedicated, what else can there be? But Paul believed that there is a lot more—because, after he told the Romans to dedicate themselves as living sacrifices, he went on to give them dozens of specific commands. Thus, dedication is necessary, but it is not a replacement for gradual spiritual growth in one area after another. Rather, dedication has to do with one's general attitude and aspiration.

When we dedicate ourselves to the Lord, we are indicating our desire and intent to live for him. But that does not mean that we can expect to fulfill the specific commands of the New Testament easily and automatically just because of our dedication. On the one hand, if we are not dedicated—that is, if we do not want to live for the Lord—we will not grow. On the other hand, dedication makes it possible for us to grow but it is not a guarantee of growth.

Spirituality, like dedication, has to do with one's basic attitude and desire to please the Lord. We can say that a person is completely spiritual, or completely dedicated, but nowhere near completely mature. Again, after Paul told the Ephesian believers to be filled with the Spirit, he went on to give them dozens of specific commands. The filling of the Holy Spirit becomes real only as we obey the specific commands of the Lord.

Dedication and spirituality can be likened to the sails of a sailboat, the distant shore can be likened to the goal of Christlikeness, and movement across the water can be likened to spiritual growth. If the sails are not up, no progress will be made. When the sails are fully up, gradual progress will be made as long as the sailor stays on the job and does his part. He will never take credit for the wind, but he will do his part in order to make use of the power of the wind.

WHAT MUST THE BELIEVER DO TO GROW?
The believer must do something in order to grow. The things he must do can be described in various ways, but they all refer to the same basic action on the part of the believer. He must obey the Lord. He must apply the Word of God in his life. He must yield to the influence of the Holy Spirit. Obviously, all of these work together. They all involve a *positive response* to God, that is, a *decision* to do what God has said he should do.

Assuming that a Christian wants to grow (in other words, he is spiritual, or dedicated) and assuming he knows what God wants him to do in some specific area of his life, all he needs to do to grow in that specific area is to respond positively by doing what he knows he should do. But there are many other things which, even though they are not requirements for growth in a certain area, are needed (some more than others) in the overall picture if the believer is going to continue to grow. These include regular Bible input, a discipler (teacher and model), prayer, fellowship with other believers, worship, and the challenge of Christian service (especially evangelism).

THE CHRISTIAN WORKER'S CHARACTER AND ATTITUDES

 PRINCIPLE 4: The Christian worker's character and his attitudes toward people are of utmost importance, even more than his talents or formal training.

We are using the phrase "the Christian worker" to refer to a wide variety of Christians, including parents, teachers, pastors, evangelists, missionaries, disciplers, Christian education directors, youth and children's workers, administrators, church music directors, seminary and Christian college professors—anyone who ministers to others. The basic goals of all these workers are the same. So are the basic principles that apply to their work. The daily activities and particular means employed by each one may differ, but such differences are relatively superficial. The core of each ministry is the same. One consideration at the core of every kind of ministry is the quality of the person who is doing the ministry. His character and his attitudes toward other people, more than his talents or formal training, will determine the effectiveness of his ministry.

CHARACTER

What qualifications must a Christian worker have? Obviously, he must be a genuine Christian. He must be at least somewhat grown up in many areas of his life, and continuing to grow spiritually.

Two particular areas of growth seem to be especially crucial in light of the significance of the Bible and the Holy Spirit, as discussed under Principle 1. First, he must have a good grasp of the Bible's teachings. This is not to say that he must be a walking Bible encyclopedia; but he should be quite familiar with both Old and New Testaments, know an accurate interpretation of the Bible's main teachings, and have a well-integrated view of God, man, and life. Paul told the young minister, Timothy, to be one "who correctly handles the word of truth" (2 Tim. 2:15). Second, he must live what he knows. He should consistently exemplify the Christian walk which comes from applying the Bible's teachings in the power of the Holy Spirit. Paul told the young minister, Titus, "in everything set them an example by doing what is good" (Titus 2:7).

THE ATTITUDE OF EMPATHY

Empathy is not the same as sympathy. Sympathy involves feeling the same feelings another person has. Thus, sympathy is mainly an emotional thing. But empathy is mainly cognitive. Empathy involves understanding another person *from the other person's point of view.* Notice how the Bible discusses this idea of empathy, even though the word is not explicitly used in these passages:

"Each of you should look not only to your own interests, but also to the interests of others" (Phil. 2:4).

"Remember those in prison as if you were their fellow prisoners, and those who are mistreated as if you yourselves were suffering" (Heb. 13:3).

The Indian saying, "Walk a mile in my moccasins," expresses the same idea. We must strive to identify with any individual we are trying to help by putting ourselves in his place. We must realize what it would be like to face life having his background, his abilities or lack of abilities, and his circle of friends. Without empathy we won't have genuine sensitivity to others. Without empathy we cannot truly apply the golden rule (Matt. 7:12; Luke 6:31; 1 Cor. 10:24), because the application of the golden rule requires us to identify with others. Perhaps this is one of the reasons James advised us to be "quick to listen, slow to speak and slow to become angry" (James 1:19). Listening is the first step toward empathy.

THE ATTITUDE OF A SERVANT

Jesus drew a contrast for his disciples in order to help them understand an attitude they should not have, and an attitude they should have: "The rulers of the Gentiles lord it over them, and their high officials exercise authority over them. Not so with you. Instead, whoever wants to become great among you must be your servant, and whoever wants to be first must be your slave—just as the Son of Man did not come to be served, but to serve, and to give his life as a ransom for many" (Matt. 20:25-28; see also Luke 22:24-27 and 1 Pet. 5:1-3).

The Christian worker is always looking for ways he can serve others, not for ways they can serve him. This is not normal, for by nature people tend to look out only for their own good. But it is the way Jesus both commanded and exemplified. "Christ Jesus . . . being in very nature God . . . made himself nothing, taking the very nature of a servant" (Phil. 2:5-7). Paul used Jesus' example to illustrate his command: "In humility consider others better than yourselves" (Phil. 2:3).

(Some have mistakenly thought that Paul in this verse commands us to have the lowest possible self-esteem. But if we examine the context, especially Jesus' example in the following verses, we will see what Paul's intent is. Paul is telling us to consider serving others more important than serving ourselves.)

Everything the Christian worker does is aimed at serving others by meeting their needs. In fact, the concept of meeting needs is one of the most basic concepts in all Christian ministries. Paul said that everything we say should be "helpful for building others up according to their needs" (Eph. 4:29).

What a contrast this is to the person who appears to minister to others, but is actually ministering more to himself, his underlying (and probably subconscious) motives completely selfish. He may enjoy the feeling of power he gets from his position of authority or leadership, or his ego may need the praise and public recognition that often comes with the more visible, "up front" kinds of ministries. Any motive that serves the needs of the minister more than the needs of the one being ministered to is out of place. The Christian worker must view himself as a servant and must desire to meet the needs of others.

THE ATTITUDE OF A GENTLE GUIDE

Jesus said, "I am gentle" (Matt. 11:29). Paul said, "We were gentle among you" (1 Thess. 2:7). Paul also said that the pastor, or overseer, must be gentle (1 Tim. 3:3). The forceful individual often bruises and discourages others, but gentleness shows a deep respect for, and a sensitivity to, each individual.

Gentleness should not be confused with weakness. Being gentle is not the same as being timid or lacking initiative. Many times the Christian worker must step forward and be bold, but always with great consideration for the impact his words and actions have on others.

He does not view others as objects to be used or manipulated. Rather, he views others as worthy of his service, and his service is to *guide* them. Sometimes our organizational structures work against us. We often work in a hierarchy of various levels of positions and authority. All this makes it easy for the worker to think of himself more as a boss than as a gentle guide. But if the Holy Spirit, from his high position and authority, can still function as a guide (John 16:13), we should do the same.

All of these attitudes are summarized in the word "love," the love shown us by God. "God so loved the world that he *gave* . . ." (John 3:16). Likewise, our motivation and attitudes toward others must grow out of the kind of love that gives.

THE "CALL"

Are people called into Christian work? Yes, every Christian is responsible to evangelize the lost and to edify the saved. Christian service is part of Christian living.

Are some called into full-time Christian work in certain special vocations such as the pastorate and missions? That depends on how you define the call. The Lord does give some service gifts to certain Christians that he does not give to others. Also, some Christians find themselves in circumstances which allow them to devote more of their time to Christian ministries than others can. And the Lord gives individualized leading to those who are obedient to him and open to his will, leading some into certain full-time Christian vocations and leading others elsewhere. One or several of these factors can be considered a call. But today there is no special call which comes as a direct revelation, as there was for the Old Testament prophets and for the Apostle Paul. If there were such a call, we would expect to find it mentioned in at least one of the three lists of qualifications for elders (pastors) and deacons in the local church (1 Tim. 3:1-7, 8-13; Titus 1:5-9). Some who mistakenly believe in such a call assume that whoever is called in this manner is automatically qualified. Because of this mistake, some enter into full-time Christian positions who are unqualified, while others who are qualified fail to follow the Lord's leading into a full-time Christian position because they have not gotten the "call." This view ignores the abundant teaching of the New Testament on the subject of the character and attitudes of the Christian worker.

TWO
THE INDIVIDUAL, THE BENEFICIARY OF CHRISTIAN MINISTRY

PRINCIPLE 5
The Inner Person

PRINCIPLE 6
Cognition and Organismic Needs

PRINCIPLE 7
Self-control, Values, and Self-concept

THE INNER PERSON

 PRINCIPLE 5: The inner person functions in three distinct ways: intellectually, emotionally, and volitionally. Sensory input stimulates these inner functions which in turn govern one's conscious actions.

While many philosophers and psychologists believe that a human being is entirely physical, the Bible clearly teaches that man is more than that. Man was created in the image of God, who is spirit (Gen. 1:27; John 4:24). Thus, man must have a spirit as well as a body. This spirit is completely nonmaterial and can exist apart from the material body, although the body is not alive without the spirit (2 Cor. 5:1-8; James 2:26). While body and spirit are together, the spirit is able to govern the conscious actions of the body, *perhaps* through the cerebral cortex of the brain.

When the Bible refers to the nonmaterial part of a human being, it uses a variety of words including heart, mind, affections, soul, spirit, and will. These are not separate and distinct entities within a human being.

Rather, they are simply different ways of referring to the nonmaterial part of man, which we will call the "inner person."

These various biblical words are sometimes used interchangeably and sometimes used to distinguish particular inner functions, but they are never used explicitly to differentiate between distinct inner essences or entities.

In this section we will analyze the functions of the inner person. In the next two sections we will use this analysis in order to derive some very important and practical principles of Christian ministry.

THREE INNER FUNCTIONS

Human beings have three basic kinds of internal functions, as indicated on the diagram below. (This diagram is admittedly an oversimplification of a

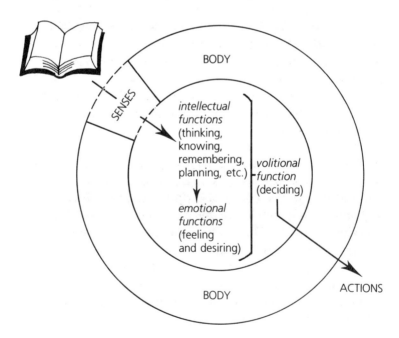

complex subject. Nevertheless, it is best to begin with a simple analysis and refine it later.) The *intellectual functions* include recognizing, thinking, understanding, knowing, remembering, establishing a system of beliefs and a system of values, evaluating, planning, and imagining. The *emotional functions* include all sorts of feelings, desires, and motives such as sorrow, happiness, hate, love, anger, sympathy, fear, and satisfaction. The *volitional function* is the function of the will, that is, choosing or deciding.

These three areas, the intellectual, emotional, and volitional, are three areas of *function* of the inner person, not three separate internal entities. Therefore, instead of saying that the intellect thinks, or that the emotions feel, or that the volition decides, it is more accurate to say that the *person* thinks, feels, and decides. It is always dangerous to break up the inner person in such a way that more than one center of responsibility results, as we do when we claim that our intellect told us to do one thing but our emotions told us to do something else. Such talk is a cop-out—a convenient attempt to avoid accountability for one's choices and actions.

Charles Ryrie makes a similar point after discussing the multifaceted nature of both the material and the nonmaterial aspects of man.

Although man is a many-faceted being . . . man is a unity and acts as one. What I do, I do, not a part of myself. It is a mistake to speak of "my old nature doing thus and so" or to say that "this stemmed from the soul and not the spirit." True, certain aspects of my being may originate an action, but that action is performed by me, not part of me. Too often when we speak like that, we tend to excuse ourselves from some evil action by relegating it to some part of our being which somehow becomes detached so that we are

relieved of responsibility. . . . I am responsible for my
actions and cannot shift the blame to some part of me
which I have tried to make not a part of me. The hand
that pulls the trigger to murder brings imprisonment or
death to the whole person. . . . No one can say that it
was merely the hand . . . that is to blame. The person is
to blame. (Balancing the Christian Life, *Chicago: Moody*
Press, 1969, pp. 32-33.)

THE CONSCIENCE

Only three functions are identified on the diagram.
Some would add the conscience as either a separate
function or a separate entity. But the conscience is
merely one of the ways the intellectual functions and the
emotional functions work together. The conscience is
nothing more than a learned bond which ties together a
particular thought with a particular feeling. For
example, the memory of a certain act, or a plan to
commit a similar act, automatically brings about a
particular negative (or positive) feeling.

The fact that our intellectual and emotional functions
can cooperate in such a manner is due to God's design.
In other words, the conscience is God-given. However,
the content of the conscience—that is, the particular
emotional reactions that are paired with thoughts about
particular acts—is not necessarily God-given. The
content of one's conscience is learned, often as a result of
childhood conditioning.

The fact that the content of the conscience is not
implanted by God can be seen in the example of the
Corinthians (1 Cor. 8:4-13). They had long believed that
their idols were real gods. When they became Christians
this previous "knowledge" (actually false knowledge)
was combined with their new knowledge of the true
God. So, when they thought of eating food that had
been offered to one of the idols, their emotional reaction
was strongly negative. This negative reaction of *their*

conscience was determined by the false knowledge that they had learned earlier in life; but for many believers the conscience would not register any negative response. So these guilt feelings were not God-given, as though God had implanted this emotional reaction in their conscience.

Since the content of the conscience is not God-given, one's unaided conscience is not necessarily a reliable monitor of right and wrong. It may be overly sensitive, as was the case with the Corinthians. Or, it may be insensitive, as is the case with the hypocrites foreseen by Paul (1 Tim. 4:2). But one's conscience can be properly "instructed" to be a more reliable monitor of right and wrong as one's understanding of the Bible increases.

INTELLECTUAL FUNCTIONS

The intellectual functions operate on various levels of awareness. Although we can possess a vast store of information, we can be consciously aware of only a small portion of that information at any one time. Conscious thoughts and experiences that are stored in the memory can be likened to black and white pictures that are dropped into a barrel. Those that were "dropped in" most recently are most easily recalled. Some experiences are more vivid than others, like color pictures, and these too are more easily recalled.

Usually, we are not able to turn our thoughts on and off. Rather, what we are consciously thinking about depends on what experience we are currently having and upon what our senses are focused. In fact, it is almost impossible to stop thinking, or to clear the mind. If we want to get rid of one thought, we must replace it with another thought. The last thought in our mind is in our consciousness until another one replaces it.

The intellect, then, has two distinctive features which

set it apart from the other inner functions. First, many of our thoughts come directly from our experience and sensory input. Second, the intellect can store many ideas, but only a few of these ideas will be in our conscious awareness at any one time. Our emotions are quite different.

EMOTIONAL FUNCTIONS

Our emotions are positive and negative reactions to whatever thoughts are consciously being considered at any given moment. We do not emote just to emote. For example, if we are going to cry genuinely, we will cry *about something*. If we are going to be happy, we will have something which makes us feel happy. In other words, emotions do not occur in isolation; they are always a reaction to some intellectual activity (some observation or some recollection).

Also, emotions are not stored. Instead, they are "of the moment." A sad memory may evoke a sad emotional response every time it is recalled to consciousness, but it is the memory which is stored, not the emotion. Emotions are always for the nonce.

THE SEQUENCE

Because of what we know about the intellectual functions and the emotional functions, we can determine the sequence in which the three inner functions always occur. As indicated on the diagram: first, something in the environment is sensed. It is seen or heard or detected with one of the other senses. The individual becomes aware of that thing. This awareness is an intellectual function which can be stored and recalled later. Then the individual responds to it emotionally, either positively or negatively. Next, based on what the person is aware of and how he feels about it, he makes a decision, which in turn leads to action. Thus, there is input, then personal operations (intellectual, then emotional, then volitional) based on that input, and finally output. Or, in other words, there is *impression, personal functions,* and *expression.*

Here is a simple illustration which may help you understand this sequence:

1. There is a book sitting on a bookstore shelf.
2. You *see* the book.
3. You are *aware* of the book's existence and title (which happens to be *How to Get Rich Without Trying*).
4. You have a strong *desire* to find out how to do this.
5. You *decide* to buy the book.
6. You *buy* the book.

Or, consider this illustration:

1. There is fruit on the tree, and a "snake in the grass."
2. The woman *sees* the fruit on the tree and *hears* the lies of Satan.
3. She *thinks* that, if she eats the fruit, she will not die, but instead she will become like God.
4. She is *pleased* by the sight of the fruit and *desires* to be as wise as God.
5. She *decides* to eat the fruit.
6. She *eats* the fruit (Gen. 3:1-6).

This sequence could be illustrated many times over, both from Scripture and from our common experiences, but it is always the same: impression, three personal functions, expression. Or, in more psychological terms: stimulus, organism, response.

GAINING ACCESS TO THE INNER PERSON

As ministers and workers we would like to be able to influence an individual directly in his inner person. However, we are quite limited in what we can do. The only entrance we have into the inner person is through the senses. (That is, the only entrance we have into the *conscious* inner person is through the senses. While such devices as drug therapy, hypnosis, and behavioral conditioning can have some effect on the inner person as his behavior is being manipulated, they are severely limited when it comes to true education or ministry.) So, for all practical purposes, our influence on a person must "get through" to his inner person through his senses, especially the senses of seeing and hearing. And thus the functions of the inner person which we can influence most directly are the intellectual functions.

But the Holy Spirit does not have this same limitation. For one thing, he is not available to be sensed in the same way that we are. A person's senses are designed to receive stimuli from the physical environment. That physical environment includes us, but it does not include the Holy Spirit since he is a spirit. The Holy Spirit, rather than being sensed by the individual as we are, has direct access to every area of the individual's inner person. He can directly influence his thinking, his emotions, and his decisions. This does not mean that the Holy Spirit *does* in fact give him information directly, or produce certain emotional reactions directly, or make decisions for him. It only means that he *can* do so. As we will see later in our discussion of evangelism, the Holy Spirit influences people directly, but never overrides their inner functions. In other words, the Holy Spirit never forces anyone to think, feel, decide, or act a certain way. Human freedom of thought and action is one of God's highest priorities, and it should be one of ours also.

COGNITION AND ORGANISMIC NEEDS

 PRINCIPLE 6: Cognition is basic, but organismic needs are more powerful in stimulating an individual's behavior. We should respond positively to an individual's organismic needs.

In the previous section we analyzed the individual's inner functions. In this section we take another look at the intellectual and the emotional functions.

THE IMPORTANCE OF COGNITION

The word "cognition" refers to the intellectual functions. Cognition must take place for anything else to happen in the inner person. Yet, cognition alone is inadequate. Cognition should often lead to decision and action.

Some people, in view of the fact that cognition by itself is insufficient, emphasize those things which should follow cognition—emotions, decisions, and especially actions. In fact, sometimes they emphasize them so much that they end up downgrading cognition. "The Lord doesn't want you to sit and talk," they might say. "He wants you to get out and witness." "Why waste four years getting an education when you could be serving the Lord?" "Don't try to understand it; just take it by faith and act upon it." These are lopsided statements which devalue cognition.

Although cognition is extremely important, it should not be valued as an end in itself. Cognition is first in the sequence of inner functions, so it is the prerequisite to everything else that the person does. And it is not merely the awareness of isolated facts which makes cognition a basis for action. Cognition also involves the interrelating of facts, ideas, assumptions, and much more. As facts and ideas are compared and integrated, we gain new insight into life and the universe. We begin to see the dynamics and principles which account for those isolated facts and experiences. We evaluate viewpoints, we test presuppositions, we establish priorities in a value system. All of these serve as a check on emotions and as a guide for decision and action. The action, whether it is witnessing or serving or whatever, is always done better if it is guided by careful and thorough thought. Cognition is central to both evangelism and edification, and instruction is logically the most basic of all the elements in the life of the local church. Doctrine and education *are* important!

But, of course, there is the opposite error, which is the glorification of cognition. We make this mistake in many of our churches by focusing all of our attention on doctrine and none on action. What we need is balance. We need a healthy emphasis on cognition. We also need to remind ourselves that Christianity is more than knowledge; it is also a way of life.

OUR EMOTIONS

All people emote. We were created to have emotional reactions to our conscious thoughts. Emotions, however, can work against us. General anxiety and depression interfere with many people's lives. Fears can turn a pleasant day into a terrible experience or lead to defense mechanisms and irrational behavior. But perhaps the most widespread emotional disorder of all is the lack of control of one's desires or motives. This disorder may even be universal.

Learning to control one's emotions seems to be a long and difficult task. Children soon find out that they cannot have everything they want whenever they want it, so the struggle begins. We, as Christian workers, can help people gain control over their emotions. But in order to do so, we must be aware that there are two different kinds of desires or motivations. One kind stems from the fact that we are human. That is, some of our desires are simply part of God's design. These desires are called organismic needs and are discussed in the remainder of this chapter. The other kind stems from the fact that we are sinners. These desires, which grow out of our basic selfishness, are discussed in the next chapter.

ORGANISMIC NEEDS

"Organismic needs" (a phrase used in the fields of biology and psychology) refers to the needs that are built into the nature of an organism, whether it is a plant, a simple animal, a more complex animal, or a human being. All that an individual organism needs to survive and be healthy are its organismic needs. Even though we are limiting our discussion to human beings, we will still use this phrase in order to emphasize the fact that these needs are inherent in human life. In other words, we have these needs because God designed us in such a way that these needs are a necessary and integral part of our humanness.

Organismic needs are quite different from normative needs. In fact, it is unfortunate that the word "needs" has to be used in both phrases, because psychologically and educationally normative needs and organismic needs are oceans apart. Normative needs are not built in. Instead, they are based on norms that are established by someone or something outside the individual. When a mother says to her son, "You need to polish your shoes," she is setting up a standard or norm which does not come from inside the boy. Our need to pay taxes comes from the structure of our society and from our government, not from within us as individuals. Many other standards are established for people by their parents and by civil government. And many are established by God, such as the need to resist temptation, the need to be patient and honest, and the need to bear one another's burdens. But these are all normative needs.

This distinction between organismic and normative needs is very significant for the Christian worker because he will constantly be faced with both kinds of needs. But they operate very differently. On the one hand, organismic needs are built in and often subconscious. Yet they automatically motivate a person to action. (This is why psychologists also call them inner drives, because they drive people to whatever actions they think will satisfy the needs.) On the other hand, normative needs are not built in and they do not automatically motivate a person.

Below is a list of organismic needs grouped into three categories. The physical needs pertain to the individual's body and its functions. The social needs pertain to the individual's relationship to other individuals. The personal needs, or ego needs, pertain to the individual and his need to think well of himself.

ORGANISMIC NEEDS (INNER DRIVES)

Physical	Social	Personal
air	security	self-actualization,
food	acceptance, belonging	accomplishment,
water	being understood	progress
activity	companionship	new experiences
rest	recognition	knowledge, understanding
safety	love, affection	order, beauty
sex	praise, approval	

Depending on the circumstances, the physical needs are often the strongest motivators, the social needs are next in strength, and the personal needs are weakest. The average person in our culture routinely has most of his physical needs met. Thus, his daily activities are motivated mainly by his social and personal needs. In many of the more primitive cultures, daily activity is much more motivated by the needs for food and safety.

If you want to increase both your understanding of yourself and your understanding of how organismic needs work, you might try carrying a list of social and personal needs with you for a few days and keeping a record of your own activities and what needs are motivating those activities. You will probably find (if you are able to be honest enough with yourself) that there are certain needs which motivate you repeatedly, while other needs seldom do. Each individual has a different personality, a different background, a different set of daily circumstances, so each individual has his own unique set of needs which are his main drivers.

It is somewhat more dangerous to try to analyze other people's motives or to try to predict their behavior. It is difficult enough to be sure of one's own motives, let alone someone else's. Since certain activity might spring from one motive for one individual but from a different motive for another individual, it would be dangerous to assume that a certain activity always reveals a certain underlying motive.

RESPONDING TO AN INDIVIDUAL'S ORGANISMIC NEEDS

We must remember that these organismic needs are built in and God-given. They were designed into human nature, so there is nothing morally good or bad about the needs themselves. Rather, the way a person goes about meeting his needs can be good or bad, but the needs themselves are morally neutral.

The desires that arise from these needs are also neutral, and we should do what we can to help meet these needs in legitimate ways. It is a serious mistake to ignore organismic needs or to tell a person that he should deny his desires and needs. If we cannot meet his needs, he will be driven to find someone or something else that will meet them. Besides the fact that *we* can drive people away from us by our rude or critical behavior, we must also keep in mind that *their* inner needs will also drive them away from us, even if we do nothing.

Notice God's response to Adam's need for companionship (Gen. 2:18-24). God was aware of Adam's need, for he said, "It is not good for the man to be alone." The very next sentence in that passage tells us that God planned to do something to meet that need. God did not ignore Adam's need, nor did he tell Adam to deny his need. In fact, Adam was not yet aware of his own need, and God gave him the task of naming all the animals so that he would realize that he was one of a kind and needed another human being as a helper.

Organismic needs are legitimate and they are powerful motivators. Christian workers should not hesitate to meet these needs. We should make each individual feel accepted and part of the group. We should show him that we can see things from his perspective. We should be quick to offer recognition and approval whenever appropriate. We should help him see his own accomplishments. And, we should help him appreciate his own growth of knowledge and insight. Through our genuine friendship we should be responsive to each individual's inner needs.

But friendship must be genuine. If you know the motivating power of these inner drives, it is all too easy to use them in a possessive "friendship" to manipulate another person.

One more caution is necessary in connection with

motivation. Some people may be strongly drawn to us because no one else is meeting their organismic needs, and we are. For example, they may attend Sunday school class, not because they want to learn in general, and not because they want to learn the Bible in particular, but because we are the only person in their lives who makes them feel welcome. Or an individual may even go through the motions of accepting Jesus because he knows we will approve, and no one else has shown him approval for four years.

In order to guard against such unintentional manipulation, we should get to know as much as we can about a person's background. We should find out if he might be rejected by others, or if some other organismic need is consistently going unmet. Also, we should try to convey the idea to him that our friendship is not dependent upon his making certain decisions or commitments. That is, he does not have to "accept" our Jesus in order to gain our friendship.

SELF-CONTROL, VALUES, AND SELF-CONCEPT

 PRINCIPLE 7: Self-control begins with the control of sinful desires. This requires the work of the Holy Spirit, biblical beliefs, a sound value system, and a healthy view of oneself.

THE CONTROL OF SINFUL DESIRES

Even though all of our inner functions (intellectual, emotional, and volitional) are affected by the fall, sin seems to be especially hard at work in the area of the emotions. Scripture draws attention to this area when describing the sin nature. Paul speaks of "the sinful nature with its passions and desires" (Gal. 5:24). And John speaks of "the cravings of sinful man" (1 John 2:16). After all, it is not sin to know about evil. (God knows more about evil than anyone else.) But it *is* sin to desire evil. Of course, it is also sin to decide, and to do, evil. But sin seems to begin to brew in the emotions. Since an individual's emotions stimulate his will, the control of one's emotions will go a long way toward controlling one's decisions and actions. If we *want* to do what is right, we will find it much easier to *do* what is right.

Obviously, the work of the Holy Spirit is needed if we are ever going to desire good rather than evil. Our sinful nature is bent on evil, and only with divine help will we ever be able to overcome sinful desire. However, does the mere presence of the Holy Spirit automatically make all of our desires good? When we are saved and have the Holy Spirit living within us, are all of our motives pure forevermore? Certainly not, according to James. "Fights and quarrels . . . come from your *desires*. . . . You *want* something but don't get it. You kill and *covet*, but you cannot have what you want. . . . You ask with *wrong motives*, that you may spend what you get on your *pleasures*" (James 4:1-3, italics mine). The Holy Spirit does not control our emotions for us. Instead, he gives us the power to do so.

This is one of the ways the Holy Spirit preserves our freedom. He does not captivate or manipulate our emotions, just as he does not captivate or manipulate our intellect or our will. In short, he does not think, desire, or decide for us. He gives us the power to think, desire, and decide *as he would* if he were in absolute control, but leaves the thinking, desiring, and deciding up to us.

Some people equate the filling of the Holy Spirit with the control of the Holy Spirit. While it is true that we are commanded to be filled with the Holy Spirit (Eph. 5:18), his control of us does not mean that he takes away from us the responsibility of exercising self-control (Gal. 5:22, 23). When we are filled with the Holy Spirit, he works in us, enabling us to obey the Holy Spirit. We are active, not passive. We are following the Holy Spirit's influence in our lives, but are not so controlled by him that we become robots.

But if the Holy Spirit does not control our desires for us, how exactly do we control our own desires? Before we can control any particular desire we must first recognize and evaluate that desire. The acts of recognizing and evaluating are intellectual functions.

Thus, the control of the emotions begins in the intellect. Before a person can desire what is right, he must know what is right. Before a person can evaluate a sinful desire as sinful, he must know what is sin. If his beliefs are not correct, his evaluations will also be faulty. Thus, having a set of correct beliefs—that is, knowing what is truly right and wrong—is absolutely necessary for the control of sinful desires. (This is one of the reasons that instruction is logically the most basic element in the life of the local church.)

VALUES

Many people believe the right things, but their beliefs have little impact on their lives. They know the difference between right and wrong, but they don't really care. The knowledge of right and wrong is a prerequisite to the control of sinful desires, but knowledge alone, without a system of values, is rather powerless.

Beliefs are what we hold to be true. Values are what we hold to be important. When values are ranked into a *system* of values, then that value system is what we hold to be most important, and next most important, in descending order. When we have determined what our values are, we have something which can be as powerful in creating conscious motivation as the unconscious needs and desires are in creating sub-conscious motivation. For example, it is one thing to believe that honesty is right and lying is wrong. It is quite a different thing to also value honesty as one of the most important virtues. A person who values honesty will be much more likely to live honestly than the person who values other things—such as popularity or possessions—more than he values honesty.

A person's values are deep seated and not easily changed. Yet, if there is going to be any lasting improvement in a person's pattern of life, his values *must* change. One of the least effective ways to try to alter someone's value system is to give him a lecture about what should be important to him. But there are other means which are more effective to bring about value changes. Some of these other means are mentioned in later sections.

Some of the ideas discussed in this section and the previous section are included in the diagram below. This diagram is, admittedly, another oversimplification. It is meant to show some of the key features of the individual's inner dynamics and how they relate to each other and lead to his behavior. As a general rule, organismic needs *tend* to be subconscious, while one's beliefs and values *tend* to be conscious. But, of course, one's organismic needs do often become conscious, and one's value system can be made up of a number of "blind spots."

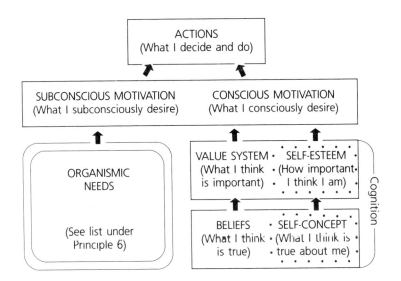

Some Christian workers focus their efforts on only two places in the above diagram—actions and beliefs. They like to see people act a certain way and believe certain things. Unfortunately, those who limit their ministries to these two areas often feel that holding the correct beliefs should automatically lead to the proper actions. But as you can see from the diagram, there is a great deal more going on within an individual that determines his behavior than just his beliefs. While it is true that beliefs form a foundation for values, and values in turn form a foundation for conscious motivation, the proper beliefs alone never guarantee the proper desires or actions. A realistic ministry will take all of the internal dynamics into account.

SELF-CONCEPT AND SELF-ESTEEM

A person's beliefs include what he believes about himself and his abilities and shortcomings. This is called his self-concept or self-image. A person's value system includes his ranking of his own worth in comparison with the worth of other people. This is called his self-esteem or self-worth. Others parts of one's beliefs and values can be relatively objective, but these two parts are the most subjective aspects of one's personality. They are also two of the most significant and powerful aspects of one's personality, and that is why they are identified separately on the diagram.

One's self-concept and self-esteem enter into virtually every thought and action. If a person's self-concept is inaccurate, his statements and behavior will seem irrational to others. If his self-concept is low (that is, if he thinks he has few abilities) he may shy away from responsibility, or rely on someone else to take the initiative. If he values himself too highly, he may treat others in a condescending and obnoxious manner, or display a false humility. If he does not value himself highly enough, he may act withdrawn or he may act aggressively and put on an air of superiority in order to compensate. If he views himself as an expert on certain subjects, that will determine the role he plays in many discussions. If he views himself as occupying a position of leadership or authority, he may treat others differently than he would otherwise. Indeed, every role and virtually every action is directly or indirectly tied into his self-concept and his self-esteem.

One of the Christian worker's most significant (and most difficult) tasks is to help another person form a healthy view of himself. A healthy self-concept and a healthy self-esteem will be positive, yet realistic. Psychologically, a person should see himself as being a capable person. Yet, he should be realistic about his weaknesses. Theologically, a person should see himself as important because he is created in God's image and because Jesus loved him enough to die for him. Yet he must be realistic about his sin nature. How an individual sees himself will have a subtle but strong effect on his self-control and his spiritual growth.

GETTING TO KNOW THE INDIVIDUAL

As Christian workers, we want to help people, which requires that we have a good general understanding of people. The various disciplines which study people, such as psychology, sociology, and counseling are all worthwhile areas of study for the Christian worker.

But we must also get to know *personally* the individuals with whom we are working. We don't really know someone if all we know about him is what he looks like, what his name is, and what he does. We must also get to know what he believes, what he thinks is important, how he views himself and his own worth, and what unconscious needs motivate him. Such intimate information is revealed only through hours and years of contact. A questionnaire alone cannot do the job. Many conversations in a nonthreatening atmosphere and many observations in informal settings are needed.

Each person has different needs, different beliefs, and different values and motivations. Our ministry must be geared to the unique aspects of each individual. The better you know each person, the more personal you can make your ministry and the more effective your ministry will be.

THREE
THE GOSPEL, THE FIRST MESSAGE OF CHRISTIAN MINISTRY

CONTENT OF THE GOSPEL

 PRINCIPLE 8: The gospel message is that Christ died for our sins and rose again. This is the message that must be presented and explained in evangelism.

When we examine various gospel tracts and other supposed presentations of the gospel, we notice that they seldom agree on the exact content of the gospel message. Some presentations of the gospel include concepts that other presentations omit. We would like to know exactly what facts an individual must be aware of, and accept as true, before he can trust Jesus Christ as Savior and obtain eternal life. But each of these presentations gives a different answer to that question. In light of this confusion we need to take a careful look at the New Testament's definition of the gospel message.

THE WORD "GOSPEL"
The word "gospel" means good news or good message. But news is never considered good unless it meets a bad situation. In one situation a certain bit of news might be

welcomed as the best thing the person has heard in a long time. In another situation that same bit of news might have the opposite effect. For example, suppose you have been working hard all day and have not had anything to eat. Then you hear someone say, "I have a sandwich and some lemonade for you." In that case, it is good news. But suppose you have just finished your annual Thanksgiving meal when you hear someone offer the sandwich and lemonade. In that situation the same news is not nearly as good. Indeed, some would consider the offer of this additional food to be quite disgusting.

The same thing is true whether the need is a physical need (such as food) or a spiritual need. How good the news sounds depends on how bad the situation seems. Thus, an individual who does not adequately grasp, or who denies, his spiritual lostness will not see the gospel as good news. Part of our job is to help him see how bad his situation is so that he can appreciate the goodness of the gospel. This means that our presentation of the gospel, in order to be a complete presentation, must include both the negative and the positive. Notice that both the negative (the bad situation of being a sinner who is separated from God) and the positive (the good news proper, Christ's substitutionary death and resurrection) are included in the next chart.

Four extended passages in the New Testament use the word "gospel" and define the content of the gospel message. They are Acts 10:36-43; Acts 13:32-39; Romans 1:1-7; and 1 Corinthians 15:1-8. A thorough study of all four passages would be very instructive, but due to space, only the last passage is discussed here.

In 1 Corinthians 15:1-8, Paul is restating the gospel message which he had previously delivered to the Corinthians in person. The heart of the passage, verses 3-5, can be condensed as follows: I gave you *the gospel,* namely, that *Christ died for our sins and rose again.*

This is Paul's definition of the gospel message.

There are four important concepts in Paul's statement of the gospel which a person must understand before the statement will make proper sense to him. They are (1) *sin*, (2) spiritual *death*, or separation from God, (3) divine *substitution*, and (4) *resurrection*. These four concepts, which come straight out of Paul's definition of the gospel, are included in the chart below.

But what if a person does not know what God is like? He will find it hard to understand these four concepts. Thus, four attributes of God are also included in the chart.

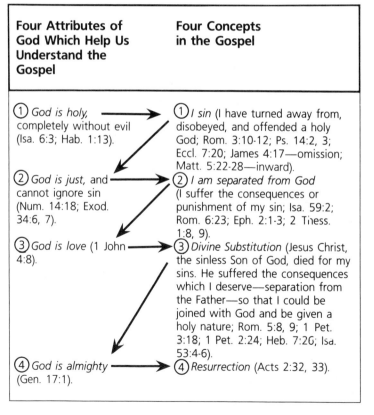

Four Attributes of God Which Help Us Understand the Gospel

Four Concepts in the Gospel

The Bad Situation

① *God is holy,* completely without evil (Isa. 6:3; Hab. 1:13).

② *God is just,* and cannot ignore sin (Num. 14:18; Exod. 34:6, 7).

③ *God is love* (1 John 4:8).

The Good News

④ *God is almighty* (Gen. 17:1).

① *I sin* (I have turned away from, disobeyed, and offended a holy God; Rom. 3:10-12; Ps. 14:2, 3; Eccl. 7:20; James 4:17—omission; Matt. 5:22-28—inward).

② *I am separated from God* (I suffer the consequences or punishment of my sin; Isa. 59:2; Rom. 6:23; Eph. 2:1-3; 2 Thess. 1:8, 9).

③ *Divine Substitution* (Jesus Christ, the sinless Son of God, died for my sins. He suffered the consequences which I deserve—separation from the Father—so that I could be joined with God and be given a holy nature; Rom. 5:8, 9; 1 Pet. 3:18; 1 Pet. 2:24; Heb. 7:26; Isa. 53:4-6).

④ *Resurrection* (Acts 2:32, 33).

Notice the logical progression indicated by the arrows. Each of the four concepts in the gospel can be properly understood only when the preceding concepts and attributes are kept in mind. When each attribute and concept is understood in order, the gospel makes perfect sense. The gospel, rather than being a mystery or a riddle, is logical and sensible.

No wonder some religions and cults have a false gospel. They have a false view of God and of sin to begin with. Since they start with false ideas, the "gospel" which they build on those false foundations is sure to be false.

In summary, Paul's definition of the gospel leads us to four concepts: sin, separation, substitution, and resurrection. These four concepts are logically linked with each other and with the attributes of God. These are the four concepts that must be presented and explained in evangelism.

PREEVANGELISM

 PRINCIPLE 9: A person often needs to change some of his basic ideas before he can begin to understand the gospel.

PREREQUISITES TO UNDERSTANDING SIN

The chart in the previous section indicates that an individual must understand that God is holy before he can understand sin properly. But there are several other concepts that a person must also understand before he can understand the concept of sin. He must understand that God exists, that God is personal, and that God is the Creator (which makes us his creatures who are responsible to him). If the individual either misunderstands or rejects any of these ideas, he cannot logically accept the biblical idea of sin.

This list of prerequisite concepts may look rather long to some of us. And some of these subjects are very involved. So how much should we discuss in our witnessing? Should we simply "stick to the gospel" as some would advise us? The answer depends upon the person with whom we are talking. If he has genuine questions about the prerequisites mentioned above, we should do all that we can to help him answer these questions. This means that the whole field of apologetics (which focuses primarily on the questions of the existence and nature of God and the reliability of the Bible) is appropriate and often necessary in evangelism. Such preliminary work, which is called preevangelism, lays the necessary foundation for evangelism proper—the presentation of the concepts of sin, separation, substitution, and resurrection.

Since some people love to argue about religious things just to have a hot debate, not really wanting to learn anything, it is important to discern whether or not the individual's questions are genuine. If they are, we have an opportunity, and an obligation, for preevangelism.

CULTURAL HINDRANCES

There may have been a time when our North American culture favored Christian evangelism more than it does now. This was the time when the concepts mentioned above were more commonly believed. When that was the case, the gospel message made sense to a person more quickly, and preevangelism was required less often than it is now. But today, the common beliefs in our culture are often the opposite of these concepts.

We cannot assume that a person who has grown up and been educated in our culture is "with you" when you discuss such topics as God, sin, and life after death. Regarding belief in God, he may well be an atheist or agnostic rather than a theist. In other words, he may have concluded that there is no God, or he may have concluded that no one can be certain whether or not there is a God. And if he does use the word "God," he may use it to refer to the impersonal forces of nature or to some mystical ultimate essence. Even if he thinks of God as a personal God, he may view him as a lenient pushover who oozes love and has a short memory. The concept of a God who is not only loving but also holy is quite rare in our society.

Regarding sin, he may well be a moral relativist, rather than holding a biblical view of right and wrong. In other words, he may believe that each individual has the right to determine for himself what is right or wrong in any given situation. Even a person who uses the word "sin" may be referring to his own relativistic and situational view of sin, or only to the gross social sins such as murder. He may call some actions sins, but on balance he would probably feel that very few people (if any) should be called sinners. This means that the bad situation (being a sinner who is separated from a holy and just God) does not make sense to many people.

Regarding life after death, he may be an evolutionist who holds that there is no personal existence after physical death. Or, he may be a reincarnationist who holds that everyone returns to earth in a different body in an ongoing cycle of earthly lives.

These and other views commonly held in our culture make evangelism more difficult. We have a responsibility to be aware of the common beliefs of our culture and to be able to respond to them intelligently so that we can pave the way for the presentation of the gospel.

WITNESSING WITH BIBLICAL AUTHORITY

Our problem with our culture is even deeper than suggested in the previous section. Even our source of information is not recognized. We can expect many people to look at us rather funny when we use the Bible as our authority. Many twentieth-century people feel that theirs is the only enlightened generation. Thus, anyone who lived before the twentieth-century is categorized as ignorant and superstitious. And since the

Bible was written long ago, they easily lump the Bible into that same category, as an ancient book which is good only for musty scholars and quite irrelevant to anyone alive today.

Others may belong to a religious group which has substituted another book for the Bible. Still others may be existentialists who recognize no authority outside themselves. The truth-of-the-moment and the reality of subjective experiences are the only valid "authority" existentialists recognize.

Some Christians assume that they can add a persuasive punch to their witnessing by starting with, "The Bible says." But when they identify the Bible as the source of their message they automatically discredit their message for many groups of people. The Holy Spirit does convict people of sin, righteousness, and judgment (John 16:8). If we communicate the gospel message clearly and answer questions carefully, the Holy Spirit will be faithful in convicting, whether or not the individual knows that the Bible is the source of our message.

Witnessing with biblical authority is accomplished when the message is accurate and clear, when the evangelist's pattern of life exemplifies and supports the message, and when the witnessing is done in the context of prayer and love. It is not necessary to begin every sentence with "the Bible says" in order to have biblical authority in our evangelism.

SPIRITUAL SUBSTITUTION

 PRINCIPLE **10: Jesus' spiritual death was the true substitution, which is the heart of the gospel.**

JESUS—OUR SUBSTITUTE

The Apostle Peter said that "Christ died for our sins once for all, the righteous for the unrighteous, to bring you to God" (1 Pet. 3:18). Thus, Jesus was our substitute. We need to discuss the idea of substitution in general in order to appreciate the way in which Jesus qualified as our substitute.

What qualifications must any substitute have? We will call the substitute "X" and the thing for which it is substituting we will call "Y." If X is going to make a valid substitution for Y, then X must have these three qualifications:

1. X must be basically similar to Y,
2. X must be different from Y in one crucial way, and
3. X must actually stand in for, or take the place of, Y.

Suppose that an incandescent light bulb burns out in one of our living room lamps. We need another light bulb to substitute for the one that burned out, but it must meet the three qualifications listed above. First, it must be similar to the light bulb that burned out. A guitar, spoon, popsicle stick, or wastebasket will never do. Not even a catsup bottle is suitable. In fact, not every light bulb will do. It can't be a fluorescent light bulb. Nor do we want a heat bulb. And a Christmas tree light would not fit in the socket. Obviously, it must be a light bulb that is *similar* to the one that burned out.

But it should not be *identical*. A light bulb that is identical would also be burned out, so it would fail to meet the second qualification. If it is going to be a valid substitute, it must have that *crucial difference*. In fact, whatever it is that makes a substitution needed in the first place, that is the way in which the substitute must be different. A substitute for a sick teacher must be well. A spare tire must not be flat. And a replacement bulb must not be burned out.

Third, there must be an *actual exchange*. The substitute must take the place of the original item. It may meet the first two qualifications and thus be a potential substitute, but it is not an actual substitute until it stands in the place of the original item.

Jesus not only qualifies as our substitute; he is our actual substitute. First, he was similar to us because he was fully human (Heb. 2:10-18). Second, he was different from us at the crucial point because he was sinless (2 Cor. 5:21). This, of course, is the reason that a substitution is needed in the first place. If man had not sinned he would not need a savior. But since we have sinned we need a savior who is without sin to be our substitute. Third, he must take our place. Jesus took our place when he died for us. He identified with sinful man, was treated by the Father at his death as though he was a sinful man, and thus he suffered the consequences of sin for us—spiritual separation from the Father (Rom. 5:8; 1 Pet. 2:24; Isa. 53:4-6).

JESUS' SPIRITUAL DEATH WAS THE
TRUE SUBSTITUTION

Jesus died in our place, but which death of Jesus was the true substitution? Was it his physical death or his spiritual death? In order to help answer this question, we must look at the consequence of sin.

The consequence of sin is death (Rom. 6:23), but again there are two kinds of death. One kind is rather obvious, physical death, which is the separation of the inner person (soul/spirit) from the body (James 2:26). The other kind of death is spiritual death, which is the separation of the person from God.

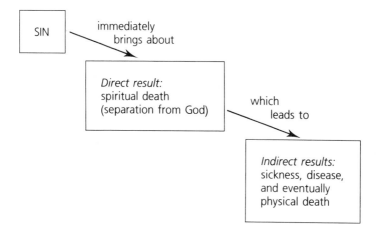

For example, when Adam sinned he did not immediately die physically, but he did immediately die spiritually. God told Adam that when he ate from the tree of the knowledge of good and evil he would die (Gen. 2:17). And Adam did die when he ate of the tree, but it was a spiritual death. Man had to hide from God (Gen. 3:8) and was banished from the Garden of Eden (Gen. 3:23). Thus, man was alienated, or separated, from God; but he was still alive physically. Adam did not die physically until hundreds of years later (Gen.

5:3-5). The spiritual death was the direct result of sin. The physical death came later as an indirect result of sin.

Since the primary or direct consequence of sin is spiritual death, we would expect that this would be the point at which Jesus would substitute for us by suffering our spiritual death for us. And this is exactly what happened. Notice that Jesus was separated from the Father when he cried, "My God, my God, why have you forsaken me?" (Matt. 27:46). Thus, at this point Jesus died *spiritually.* And what exactly did this spiritual death of Jesus accomplish for us? Jesus suffered spiritual separation from the Father so that we would not have to suffer it any longer. This is the heart of the gospel message. This is the message that Paul said was "of first importance: that Christ died for our sins" (1 Cor. 15:3).

Jesus' spiritual death on our behalf made it possible for us to be reunited with God. Notice again the wording of 1 Peter 3:18, "Christ died for sins once for all, the righteous for the unrighteous, *to bring you to God*" (italics mine). And this reunion with God happens immediately, as soon as a person accepts Jesus as his Savior, as the Holy Spirit comes to reside in the individual (Acts 19:1-6; 1 Cor. 6:19; 12:13).

Jesus did die physically, but his physical death was not substitutionary in itself. Certainly his physical death was *for* us in the sense that it was for our benefit. It was part of his identification with fallen man, but Jesus' physical death was not *in our place*, because Christians still suffer physical death.

This is what Jesus did for us, and it is referred to as the "work" of Jesus. But not only is the work of Jesus important (what he did), the person of Jesus is also important (who he was). While it is true that he had to be like us (human) to be a valid substitute, he was also different from us (divine) and thus he was sinless. But his divinity also qualified him to be the Savior in another way. One individual could substitute for only one other individual, but Jesus substituted for many. This was possible only because Jesus was divine and therefore unlimited. This is one of the reasons why the resurrection of Jesus is so important and is part of the gospel message. Jesus' resurrection proves his deity (Rom. 1:4; John 16:8-10). And Jesus' deity guarantees both his sinlessness and his ability to substitute for an unlimited number of persons.

RESPONSE AND RESULT

 PRINCIPLE 11: The only proper response to the gospel is to turn and trust Christ, resulting in a positive relationship with God and a potential for our spiritual growth.

THE NECESSITY OF RESPONSE

The four concepts which come from Paul's definition of the gospel can be considered the *facts* of the gospel. It is not enough merely for these facts to be true. Just because it is true that Christ died for our sins does not mean that everyone is automatically saved. God gives each individual a choice in this matter. Each one of us must make a decision in response to these facts.

REPENTANCE AND FAITH,
OR TURNING AND TRUSTING

The Bible describes the proper response to the gospel message as "repentance" and "faith," but we will use the words "turn" and "trust." The word "trust" is used here because it is exactly what the original words for "faith" and "believe" mean in such passages as John 1:12; 3:16, 18, 36; Acts 16:31; and Ephesians 2:8, 9. (Today the word "faith" is often used to refer to a nebulous hope, and "believe" is often used to refer to mere mental assent. Thus the word "trust" is preferred.) This trust must be an *intelligent* trust in the sense that the person must understand the facts of the gospel. This trust must also be a sincere trust because no one can fool God. A person must really want to turn from himself and his sin and want to place his trust in Jesus Christ. Furthermore, the trust has a twofold object. We trust both in Christ's person (his deity and manhood) and in his work (his suffering the consequences of sin in our place).

Repentance involves an intellectual, emotional, and volitional response. One must have the knowledge that he has done something wrong. He must also have a sorrow for the wrong done, which brings about a turning from one thing to another, the volitional response. So when a person repents, he changes the object of his trust; he decides to stop trusting one thing and starts trusting another.

In a nutshell, the proper response to the gospel message is to *turn* from oneself and from sin and to *trust* in Jesus Christ and what he has done for us.

INAPPROPRIATENESS OF WORKS AS A RESPONSE

Works (good deeds done in an effort to gain favor with God) are not the way to obtain salvation. If one truly understands the gospel, he will automatically realize that he is not saved by good works. In other words, if he really understands God's absolute holiness and justice, he will realize that no amount of supposed good deeds can ever remove the problem created by even one sin. Also, if one really understands what Jesus did when he suffered for our sins, he will realize that the idea of earning one's salvation is quite out of place, since it makes the suffering of Christ unnecessary. Even if there were no Bible passages stating that works cannot save us, that fact should be obvious from the gospel itself. But, of course, the New Testament does assert repeatedly that works cannot earn salvation (Eph. 2:8, 9; Gal. 2:16). A person's continuing to believe that he must work to gain his salvation is a clue that he does not adequately understand the gospel message.

What about baptism, church membership, or "going forward" at the end of a church meeting? Obviously, a person can easily be baptized, join a church, or "walk the aisle" at an evangelistic meeting without really turning and trusting in Christ. Such things *by themselves* are inappropriate responses to the gospel. In fact, they are actually dangerous responses if the person feels that they are sufficient to make him right with God.

THE RESULTS OF TRUSTING CHRIST

When a person turns and trusts in Christ, or "accepts Jesus as Savior," the primary consequence of his sin is canceled. He was separated from God, but now he has God the Holy Spirit living permanently with him. Thus, a new positive *relationship* is established. His sins are forgiven and he is now considered part of God's family.

Besides this new, positive relationship he has a new *potential*. Because of the presence of the Holy Spirit he now has divine help in overcoming his old problems. But his old problems are not automatically nor instantly solved. The solutions will come through a growth process rather than instant attainment. The process requires time and thoughtful attention.

Sometimes we will hear the statement, "Jesus is the answer." But we must be sure we know what the

question, or the problem, is. Jesus *is* the answer to our
sin problem. By accepting Jesus as Savior, we do
immediately have a new relationship with God.
Furthermore, we potentially have the answer to all our
problems. But growth depends on our choices, just as
the decision to accept Christ is a choice we must make.
Growth is not automatic, nor is it forced on us. When
we do grow, it may well be a result of the influence of
Christian friends, Christian teachers and counselors, and
the Christian "therapy" group—the functioning church.
With these considerations in mind it is legitimate to say
that Jesus is the answer. But it is not legitimate to say
that Jesus is the instant, automatic answer to all our
problems, if by saying that we imply that we have no
responsibility for our own Christian life and growth.

A COMPLETE PRESENTATION

 PRINCIPLE 12: The gospel presentation must be complete. A complete presentation is based on an adequate understanding of the sin problem.

THE GOSPEL MESSAGE SUMMARIZED

The gospel message along with the proper response can be summarized in the six points listed below. Notice that the message says something first about me (this part states the problem), then about Jesus (this part states the solution), then again about me.

MY SPIRITUAL CONDITION

1. My *sin*
2. The consequences of my sin (*separation* from God)

JESUS' PERSON AND WORK

3. The *sinless* Christ
4. His suffering in my place (*substitution*)
5. His *resurrection*

MY RESPONSE

6. I *turn* (repent) and *trust* (have faith in) Christ

If an individual denies any one of the first five points, there would be no reason for him to turn to Christ. If he accepts the first five points, he will see the need to turn and trust Christ.

When we talk about responding to the gospel message, we must remember that we are talking only about man's part. We recognize that no one comes to Christ unless the Holy Spirit has already begun to work in the person's life.

ONLY ONE PLAN OF SALVATION

We have just outlined or summarized the Bible's teachings regarding *the* gospel message and *the* proper response to that message. There is only one gospel, only one Savior, and only one proper response. In other words, there is only one plan of salvation (John 14:6; Acts 4:12; 1 Tim. 2:5). Although this one plan of salvation can be stated in various ways, the six *ideas* or *concepts* listed above are crucial.

But what about other religions and cults? They often have their own unique opinion of what man's problem is, and therefore their own unique plan of salvation. Some people even think that *any* way of salvation is acceptable as long as the person believing in that way of salvation is sincere. But, of course, sincerity is not enough. Anyone who believes a lie can be said to be sincere, but that does not change the lie into truth. A person can even sincerely believe that he is working for the Lord, but still not be saved (Matt. 7:21-23; Rom. 10:1, 2).

Whenever we find someone who believes in a different plan of salvation, or believes that any plan of salvation is all right, we may question whether his analysis of man's spiritual problem is correct or complete. The first two points in the gospel message are very important. One of our most crucial tasks in evangelism is to help each individual clearly understand his spiritual condition. Until a person understands the concepts of sin and separation from God, he will not properly understand the person and work of Jesus or what his response should be. If he does understand the concepts of sin and separation from God, the rest of the message will usually fall into place easily.

ADAPTING OUR PRESENTATION

The message is always the same, but the people to whom we witness are different. Thinking that the same memorized presentation will be well suited to everyone is a mistake. We do not change the message for a Jew, Roman Catholic, atheist, or cult member, but we will probably have to spend more time discussing and explaining certain parts of the gospel with some people, other parts of the gospel with other people. For example, with many Orthodox Jews and Roman Catholics, we do not need to spend a lot of time defending the ideas of God, holiness, and sin. But it may take extra effort and skill to overcome the Jew's misunderstandings of the person and work of Jesus, or the Roman Catholic's misunderstandings of the substitutionary nature of Jesus' death and the place of works in gaining salvation.

When we take a person's background and beliefs into account as we discuss the gospel with him, we are more likely to be able to gear our explanation so that it will make sense to him. Thus, we do not alter the content of the gospel message, but we should adjust the way we present it and what we emphasize, depending on the individual's background and beliefs.

LEVELS OF COMPLETENESS

Some gospel presentations are so shallow that they do not even qualify as genuine presentations of the gospel.

The chart below describes four levels of completeness in presenting the gospel message. It all starts with incomplete presentations of sin and the consequences of sin. If we are not specific in describing the bad situation, then our presentation of the gospel proper will not be

The Gospel Presentation

	Questions	The problem	God's solution	Individual's response
LEVEL I	1. Is there a problem?	(*Yes*, there is a problem, but little is said about it. Assumes a general dissatisfaction with life, or discouragement.)	God loves you.	(Merely to realize that God loves you.)
LEVEL II	1. & 2. Who is the *source* of the problem?	*You* do not live as you ought.	God loves you and Christ can help you.	Ask for help. —OR— Follow Jesus' example.
LEVEL III	1. & 2. & 3. What is the problem?	You *sin* and must be *punished*.	God loves you and Christ (sinless) took your punishment (substitution) (+ resurrection).	Turn (repent), and trust (faith) in Christ.
LEVEL IV	1. & 2. & 3. & 4. What is the punishment?	You sin and must be *separated* from a holy God.	God loves you and Christ (sinless) took your punishment (substitution) (+ resurrection).	Turn (repent), and trust (faith) in Christ.

specific enough either. An adequate diagnosis is necessary for an adequate cure.

This chart is organized around four questions about sin and its consequences. Level I answers only one general question. Level II answers the same question plus another question that is slightly more specific. Level III becomes even more specific by adding a third question. Level IV is the most specific because it answers all four questions. Notice that as the presentation of the problem becomes more specific and complete, the matching presentation of the solution and the response automatically becomes more complete. When presented at Level IV the gospel is well defined, but when presented at lower levels the gospel is dangerously fuzzy.

Level I is the shallowest level. Those whose message is summed up simply as "God loves you" are evangelizing at Level I. At this level little is said about any specific problem. Instead the "evangelist" happily declares "God loves you" and hopes that the listener will recognize God's love or in some way tip his hat toward God. The danger is that a person who hears a presentation at this level can have all sorts of misunderstandings about the nature of God, his own spiritual condition, and the person and work of Christ. The individual may be aware of some vague problem with life in general, but unless he goes on to find out more about his lost condition he will not be able to make an intelligent decision to accept Christ and receive eternal life.

We simply do not know at what instant a person is born again. Many people respond fully to what truth they know about Christ at a given time and later come to a fuller understanding of the meaning of salvation. It is important to remember that these initial responses to Christ are not necessarily wrong or inaccurate but that they are incomplete.

At Level II there can still be a variety of significant misconceptions in the listener's mind. Sin could be equated with ignorance or laziness by the listener. He might mistakenly feel that the help he receives from God is merely help to achieve his own selfish goals. Also, at this level he does not necessarily understand anything about God's holiness or justice, or about the person, work, and resurrection of Christ. Since he is not hearing anything specific about sin, righteousness, and judgment (compare John 16:8) or about the substitutionary death of Christ (which, after all, is the heart of the gospel), it is doubtful that he fully understands the meaning of salvation from such a shallow presentation of the gospel.

Even Level III is not as complete as it should be and might leave certain questions unanswered. For example, the listener does not need to understand that God's holiness requires a consequence of sinners being separated from him. He might still think of Jesus as dying physically for him. Or, he might even think that his present rotten life circumstances can help pay the punishment for his sins (and if that is not sufficient, self-inflicted punishment might do some good). Nevertheless, there are probably many people who come to Christ at Level III and later come to a fuller understanding.

The presentation of Level IV is the most complete. It answers many of the questions that create mis-understandings at the shallower levels. For example, if the individual clearly understands that the consequence of sin is *separation* from a holy God, and that that is the punishment Christ took for us, he will be much less likely to think that Jesus' physical death was the substitution, or that rotten life circumstances or self-inflicted punishment can be of any help.

Even a child can grasp a presentation of the gospel at Level IV easier than he can grasp a presentation at Level

III. This is because a child often understands personal (and therefore, spiritual) separation at a much earlier age than he understands physical death. Interpersonal alienation is experienced early and often by a child. In summary, a shallow, partial presentation of the gospel leaves the door wide open for many misunderstandings.

FOUR
EVANGELISM, THE FIRST PROCESS OF CHRISTIAN MINISTRY

THE PROCESS OF EVANGELISM

 PRINCIPLE 13: Evangelism should be thought of as an instructional process in which clarity is vital and in which no psychological pressure is applied.

WHAT IS EVANGELISM?

Producing converts is God's work. Evangelism is our work. We must not make the mistake of thinking that it is our job as evangelists to produce converts. Only God can save a person. Paul makes this point clear when he said, "I planted the seed, Apollos watered it, but God made it grow. So neither he who plants nor he who waters is anything, but only God, who makes things grow" (1 Cor. 3:6, 7).

This does not mean, however, that our job of evangelism is unimportant. In fact, just the opposite is true. "How can they believe . . . without someone preaching to them?" (Rom. 10:14). So we must maintain a balance. In one sense, our work of evangelism is absolutely essential because God has given us that task. In another sense, our work of evangelism is nothing because it merely opens the way for the regenerating work of God, something which only God can do.

Evangelism may be defined as *the process of explaining the gospel to the sinner and inviting him to trust Christ.* It is an instructional process which focuses primarily on the intellect rather than on the emotions. Evangelism is not a matter of sob stories, scare tactics, manipulation, or any other form of psychological pressure. Instead, evangelism focuses squarely on the intellect—it involves the clear explanation of the gospel message. As evangelists, our burden and our prayer request should be the same as Paul's: "Pray . . . that God may open a door for our message, so that we may proclaim the mystery of Christ. . . . Pray that I may proclaim it clearly" (Col. 4:3, 4).

AVOIDING PRESSURE

Of course, we do want to see results. We want to see people decide to accept Jesus as their Savior. But we must stick to our part of the job and let the Holy Spirit do his part unhindered. Our part is to inform the sinner of the facts of the gospel and invite him to trust in Christ. The Holy Spirit's job is to convict him of sin, righteousness, and judgment (John 16:8). *The most persuasive tool we have is a clear message.* If we try to add other forms of persuasion we risk getting in the way of the Holy Spirit. The Holy Spirit has a far better understanding of human psychology than we do. He also has a far better understanding of each unique individual than we do. He knows how to convict effectively, yet without overriding the freedom that the individual needs to make the decision genuinely of his own free choice.

Thus, we are not like the salesman whose livelihood depends on his volume of sales. There are very few salesmen who can afford to function merely as informers. For nearly all salesmen the goal is to make sales, and for some salesmen any means is justified by that end. The salesman's job is not done until he has closed the sale, but with the evangelist the picture is different. The evangelist has his job to do and the Holy Spirit has his. The evangelist is the one who instructs; the Holy Spirit is the one who convicts. The evangelist's job must not be confused with the Holy Spirit's job. Even though it may be difficult at times to find the fine line between a genuine invitation to trust in Christ and sales pressure, we must consciously avoid pushing a person lest we produce a psychological rather than a true spiritual conversion. (Psychological conversions are discussed under Principle 16.)

LEADING A PERSON TO TRUST CHRIST

Leading a person to trust in Christ usually takes place as the culmination of a long process of evangelism. The steps listed below are designed to emphasize two things: first, that evangelism is an *instructional process,* and second, the importance of allowing the individual opportunity for a *free, unpressured choice. After* fully explaining the plan of salvation:

1. *Check his understanding.* Does he have a clear grasp of the content of the gospel message? Be careful not to put words in his mouth. Don't merely ask him whether or not he agrees with your statements about sin, Christ, etc. Rather, let him express his understanding of the gospel in his own words.

2. If you feel that he understands, ask him, "Do you *want* to trust in Christ?" or "Do you *want* to receive Christ as your own Savior?" Be careful not to pressure him at this point. Don't think that you can do a better job of convicting him than the Holy Spirit can.

If he says no, probe further to see if there is some aspect of the plan of salvation which he still does not understand. Remind him of the seriousness of the matter and warn him of delay. Assure him you are still his friend and will keep in touch. And, of course, pray for him.

If he says he received Christ at some previous time, ask him if he is trusting Christ *now.* Whether or not he can remember the exact place and date when he received Christ is not nearly as important as whether or not he is trusting Christ right now.

If he says he wants to trust in Christ, ask him if he would like to do it now, although you should assure him that the decision can be made alone. If he says "Later, when I'm alone," ask him to tell you when he does trust Christ, and check up on him if he doesn't contact you soon. (Usually, if a person says "later," either he does not actually want to trust Christ or he is feeling some pressure. Respect his wish. Never push for a decision right now if he is not comfortable with it.) If he says "Now" (praise the Lord and) give him a *silent opportunity* to actually place his trust in Christ. (It is extremely important that you do not get in the Holy Spirit's way by saying too much. However, everyone is different, so if he needs help at this point, you might offer to word a prayer to help him express his decision, or answer any further questions, etc.)

ON-THE-SPOT FOLLOW-UP

After leading a person to trust in Christ, before you leave him:

1. Discuss assurance of salvation. Explain that assurance of salvation is not based on feelings, but on God's promises in Scripture (John 1:12; 1 John 5:11-13).

2. Answer the question, "What if I sin?" Explain that he does not lose his salvation (his being joined with God and having a new nature). However, immediate fellowship with God and many temporal benefits of

salvation are lost. For cleansing and restored fellowship, he must confess and forsake the sin (1 John 1:9; Prov. 28:13).

3. Lead him in thanking God for what God has done for him.

4. Encourage him to tell someone of his decision.

5. Discuss the importance of Bible study, Christian fellowship, and prayer. Begin to make arrangements so that he can be involved in these on a regular basis.

6. Arrange to meet with him again soon. Short-term follow-up is your responsibility. He should learn good habits of regular Bible study, Christian fellowship, and prayer directly from you.

PATIENCE, FRIENDSHIP, GENTLENESS

 PRINCIPLE 14: Evangelism includes the gradual process of building trust and cultivating friendship, but always avoids coercion.

TIME

Evangelism is a *process*. It may take a long time to gain a hearing, to clear away misconceptions, and to answer questions. Only rarely will the process be completed in the first encounter with an individual.

Suppose we are witnessing to a person who holds the common beliefs of our culture. As explained under Principle 9, hours or perhaps years of preevangelism and explanation could be required, depending on the specific background of the individual. The same is true when we are witnessing to people who belong to cults or religions which explicitly deny parts of the gospel message. This means that there are very few people to whom we could walk up and say "Christ died for our sins" and expect it to make sense. The hours of preevangelism and explanation will require much listening and patience. Thus, evangelism should not be thought of merely as a quick process of making statements. Rather, evangelism should be thought of as a long, patient process of discussion and education.

FRIENDSHIP

Rapport and warmth must be cultivated so that the individual trusts our statements and feels comfortable discussing such personal and far-reaching matters with us. In other words, meaningful evangelism takes place among friends much more easily than it does among mere acquaintances. The make-a-pronouncement-to-a-stranger approach to evangelism is the exception to the rule. Have-a-personal-discussion-with-a-friend is the rule.

This rule leads to two other suggestions. First, we should concentrate much of our witnessing among those with whom we are already friends. Second, when we have an opportunity to witness to a stranger, we ought to make every effort to become his friend so that our message will not be hindered because of a lack of the context of friendship.

We must remember that others "read" us as people besides hearing what we say. And if they don't like what they read they may close their minds to our message as well. Our message always comes to them as part of a total package, which includes our manners, integrity, habits, even our appearance and smell, and much more. Even though our message is 100 percent truth, our package may be only 40 percent friendly.

Our friendship must be natural and consistent. It dare not be the cheap, "hello, buddy" friendliness of some sales clerks who have memorized friendly sounding phrases and pasted on a smile. Such instant friendliness creates suspicion rather than trust. And if the person on the receiving end suspects us he will suspect our message too. Paul described just the opposite of this when he told of his own warm relationship with the

Thessalonians. "We loved you so much that we were delighted to share with you not only the gospel of God but our lives as well, because you had become so dear to us" (1 Thess. 2:8).

COERCION IS NEVER ACCEPTABLE

"Compel them to come in." "We persuade men." These Bible quotations and others are sometimes used to justify coercive evangelism. But these statements must be examined in their contexts and compared with other biblical teachings so that they will not be misinterpreted and misapplied in evangelism.

Did Paul *persuade* people into the kingdom? In Acts 18:13 we find this description of Paul's evangelism: "This man . . . is persuading the people." But consider the context. This statement was spoken by Jews who were attacking Paul. They did not understand that Christ had fulfilled the Jewish law by living a sinless life, and then had died for their sins. They thought Paul's message about Jesus was a denial of the validity of the law rather than a proper follow-up to the law. In short, they took Paul's message as anti-Jewish. They saw Paul as an enemy of the Jews and his evangelism as a threat to the Jewish religion. So they dragged Paul before the Roman authority, Gallio, and tried to make a case against him.

So, the statement found in verse 13 was made by Paul's enemies. They misunderstood what Paul was doing and saying, and they were trying to get him into trouble with Rome. Certainly any comment from people in such circumstances should not be considered a reliable statement about Paul's evangelism. (Of course, the passage is inspired and is therefore a completely accurate record of what went on in court and what the Jews said. But that does not mean that what the Jews said was accurate.) This passage, then, does not answer our question about Paul's evangelistic methods. We have to look elsewhere.

In 2 Corinthians 5:11, Paul himself said, "We try to persuade men." But this is not all that Paul said about himself. In 1 Corinthians 2:4 he wrote, "My message and my preaching were not with wise and persuasive words, but with a demonstration of the Spirit's power." (The same Greek word is used in both passages.) In one place Paul speaks of his evangelism as persuasive, and in another place he speaks of it as nonpersuasive, an apparent contradiction. To resolve it, we need to ask the question: In what sense was Paul's evangelism persuasive, and in what sense was it nonpersuasive? Some of the passages that we have already looked at help us answer this question. According to 1 Corinthians 3:6 and 7, we have our part to do and God has his part. According to Colossians 4:3 and 4, Paul saw his part as explaining the gospel, making it clear. According to John 16:8, God applies the "pressure" by convicting the sinner of sin, righteousness, and judgment after those concepts have been clearly presented to him by the evangelist. Paul's *message* was clear and therefore became persuasive as the Holy Spirit used it to convict the sinner; but Paul's *manner* of presenting the message was gentle. This answer is supported by other passages as well. Paul stated that it is the gospel message that has power. "The gospel . . . is the power of God for the salvation of everyone who believes" (Rom. 1:16). Notice also that Paul describes his evangelistic manner among the Thessalonians as "gentle" (1 Thess. 2:7).

One more passage will be examined here. Luke 14:23, in the New American Standard Version, contains the command, "compel them to come in." If we examine the context, we will see that this command should not be applied to evangelism. In the first place, Jesus was talking to a group of Pharisees and experts in the law at the house of one of the Pharisees (see vv. 1, 3). This fact in itself is enough to let us know that the statement "compel them to come in" is not meant to tell us how to do evangelism. After all, why would Jesus be telling the Pharisees and experts in the law how to do evangelism? In the second place, he is evangelizing *them*. The Pharisees were blindly convinced of their own righteousness, and part of Jesus' task in evangelizing them was to open their eyes to the fact that they were sinners. This is why he exposed their lack of compassion (vv. 2-6), their pride (vv. 7-11), and their selfish desire for personal gain (vv. 12-14). But one of the guests did not get the point and said, "Blessed is the man who will eat at the feast in the kingdom of God" (v. 15). No doubt, when he said this, he thought of himself as being among those who would be at that feast.

In reply, Jesus told the story of the man who prepared the great banquet, but the guest list for this banquet ended up being different from the original guest list. Certainly this story should have made the guest wonder if he really would be at that banquet. It is in the context of this story that Jesus said, "Compel them to come in." When Jesus said this, he was not telling believers how they should evangelize the lost. Nor was he using high pressure evangelism on these Pharisees. Instead, he was gently helping them see their lost spiritual condition. So, rather than supporting coercive evangelism, this passage illustrates Jesus' gentle, educational method of evangelism.

Nowhere in Scripture are we told to twist the sinner's arm. Instead, we are to present gently the truths of the gospel and let the Master Psychologist, the loving Holy Spirit, apply the pressure.

EVANGELIZING CHILDREN

PRINCIPLE 15: Evangelism of a child should begin very early, but it must be geared to the child's linguistic and mental level.

Extra caution is required when evangelizing children. For one thing, evangelists (whether parents, teachers, or pastors) sometimes try to explain the gospel to a child using the same vocabulary, symbols, and illustrations they would use if they were talking to an adult. But this is quite unfair to the child in view of his linguistic and mental limitations.

VOCABULARY

One of the child's most obvious linguistic limitations is his vocabulary. At age two a child has a vocabulary of approximately 300 words. At age three his vocabulary is around 1,000 words. It continues to increase at a rapid rate for several years. While this rapid growth in vocabulary is quite remarkable in itself, the other side of the coin is that during his earlier years there are many words which we adults use but which he has not yet learned.

Children usually will not say, "I don't understand that word." They are used to hearing many words which they don't understand. They often function on the basis of the words they do understand and pass over the others. Therefore, you should not assume that a child understands and wait for him to say so when he does not.

Another misleading practice is to ask a child if he understands what has been told him. If he gets any meaning out of the statements at all, whether it is the meaning intended or not, he will probably answer with a "yes." Even if he did not understand anything and knows it, he is still tempted to answer "yes" for a variety of psychological reasons. One obvious reason is that he wants to be grown up. So asking a child if he understands is not a safe procedure.

The most reliable way to find out if a child is understanding what he is being told is to get plenty of feedback from him in his own words. Once we get him talking to us about the gospel, we will soon be able to judge how well he understands what we have been saying. But the key here is to get the feedback in the child's own words. If he merely repeats the words we have used, we can be sure that he is a good imitator— but we cannot be sure he understands what we have said. A lecture to a child with a few headshakes or affirmative answers from him is just not enough. Instead, engage him in a genuine conversation. (More is said about communication and feedback under Principle 23.)

SENTENCE STRUCTURE
Besides the matter of vocabulary, there is also the matter of complex sentences which we adults use so frequently.

For example, suppose we want a child to memorize
2 Corinthians 5:20, or we want to explain the teachings
of this verse to him. But the verse includes these words
and phrases: "therefore," "ambassadors," "as though
God were," "appeal," "implore," "on Christ's behalf,"
and "reconciled." Note carefully, the *ideas or concepts* in
this verse are not too difficult for a child's mental ability,
but *the archaic language used to express these ideas* is
beyond his linguistic ability. A child typically learns
concrete nouns and verbs first. Other parts of speech
which perform more complicated grammatical functions
(such as prepositions, logical connectives, subjunctive
verbs, and passive voice) are not understood well by the
child until much later. And this verse contains them all!
Thus, the grammatical construction of this verse is too
complex for many children. Naturally, if the parent or
teacher explains these truths using similar grammatical
forms, that too will be beyond the ability of the child.

FIGURATIVE AND SYMBOLIC SPEECH
Besides vocabulary and sentence structure, we adults
use a great deal of figurative and symbolic speech
which is often misinterpreted by the child. Children are
much more literal in their understandings than adults
are. To a child a heart pumps blood, a shepherd cares
for real sheep, death is when you stop breathing, and
black, red, and white are simply colors. Note carefully,
the ideas and concepts behind figurative and symbolic
language are not too difficult for children, but the
figurative and symbolic form of expression may not
convey the meaning to the child. Again, the surest way
to find out if the child is understanding is to get plenty
of feedback in the child's own words.
  Besides these grammatical matters there are
various psychological pitfalls. No one is more easily
manipulated than a child. (The subtle pressures

that produce psychological conversions are discussed under the next principle.)

FOLLOW-UP

After you have led a child to Christ, follow him up the same way you would follow up any new Christian, with one addition. Get his parents involved (assuming they are Christians). In the case of a new believer who is an adult, the responsibility for follow-up, either to do it or see that it gets done, falls on the person who led him to trust Christ and, as time goes on, increasingly on the church as a whole. In the case of a new believer who is a teen or a child, the responsibility falls on the person who led him to trust Christ and on the parents.

SIMPLIFYING THE GOSPEL

How much of the gospel must a child understand? Can he get saved if we water down the gospel? We need to simplify the message for the child, but we do not simplify it by leaving parts of it out. Rather, we simplify it by communicating the gospel in words and sentences he can understand, by using illustrations that come from his limited experiences rather than from ours, and by avoiding figurative and symbolic expressions. He does not need to repeat the six points of the plan of salvation just as they are worded under Principle 12, but he does need to grasp each of the six ideas. Children can understand the gospel at a surprisingly young age *if* we are able to communicate it to them on their level.

THE AGE OF ACCOUNTABILITY

When does a child become accountable for his own decisions and actions? We know that accountability depends on knowledge. In other words, a person is held responsible (punishable) only when he knows that his act is wrong (or, when he omits an act that is within his ability and he knows that it is right). If he does not know right from wrong, he is not accountable. The fact that accountability is dependent on knowledge is taught or implied in such passages as James 4:17; Deuteronomy 1:39; Romans 4:15; and 5:13.

So, if we can find out the age at which a child can understand the difference between right and wrong, we can assume that also to be the age at which he is accountable. We can also assume that at the same age he is able to understand the plan of salvation. (Certainly a child cannot understand the plan of salvation before he can distinguish right from wrong, since the first point in the gospel has to do with sin. Also, it would seem strange if a child's understanding of the plan of salvation were delayed until some time after he could tell right from wrong, because then he would be accountable but not yet able to be evangelized.)

Thus, the central question is, At what age does a child know right from wrong? Many psychologists (including Sigmund Freud, Eric Eriksen, Robert Havighurst, Jean Piaget, and Lawrence Kohlberg) agree that a child's ability to tell right from wrong, that is, his conscience or super ego, begins to function quite early— perhaps during the late preschool years or very early school years. This means that the age of accountability occurs perhaps as early as age four, five, or six for many children. Rarely, a precocious child might attain the age of accountability earlier than this. Occasionally, a child's age of accountability might be delayed beyond these ages due to parental training or example which confuses the child's understanding of right and wrong. Obviously, since accountability depends on knowledge, those who suffer mental retardation become accountable according to what they are able to understand.

PSYCHOLOGICAL CONVERSIONS

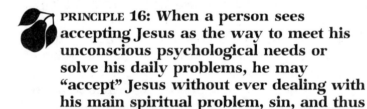 **PRINCIPLE 16: When a person sees accepting Jesus as the way to meet his unconscious psychological needs or solve his daily problems, he may "accept" Jesus without ever dealing with his main spiritual problem, sin, and thus not really be saved.**

Many conversions are psychological rather than spiritual. In a spiritual conversion, the person is spiritually born again. In a psychological conversion the person goes through the motions of receiving Jesus or does something which we often associate with receiving Christ (praying a certain prayer, going forward at an evangelistic meeting, etc.) but is never really saved.

There are two common causes of psychological conversions: pressure, and confusion over the results of sin.

PSYCHOLOGICAL CONVERSIONS
CAUSED BY PRESSURE

Everyone is a possible victim of a con artist. Because of our organismic needs, fears, and desires we are all vulnerable to psychological manipulation. Of course, the con artist purposely manipulates others, but our concern here is with the evangelist who *unknowingly* pressures another person into a psychological conversion.

The evangelist may be a zealous preacher, an eager camp counselor, or even a loving parent. None of these people wants to create a false conversion, but it happens anyhow, partly because interpersonal dynamics are so complex, so subtle, and so powerful. We all affect others in ways of which we are not aware. When those everpresent interpersonal dynamics become so strong that a person makes a "decision" to accept Jesus because of the psychological dynamics rather than because of the conviction of the Holy Spirit, he has been unintentionally conned into thinking he is saved.

Admitting that psychological conversions do take place within Christianity may not be easy for many Christians. It is relatively easy for Christians to draw upon psychological explanations when they set out to analyze conversions to other religions or cults. But we must recognize the fact that an individual does not set aside his psychological needs and fears just because he is considering Christ. We dare not oversimplify the matter by assuming that all conversions to other religions and cults are psychological, while all conversions to Christ are spiritual. Indeed, it may be that many more "conversions" to Christ are psychological than we would ever guess! Certainly there are many genuine, spiritual conversions to Christ. Perhaps even a large majority of conversions to Christ are genuine. But we must be alert to the possibility of false conversions and do everything we can to avoid psychological manipulation. One of our most crucial tasks is to begin to recognize the ways in which we *unconsciously* manipulate others.

Suppose, for example, that a teenager has been rejected by his parents and peers. His real underlying motivation (his need for acceptance) is unconscious, but it is still strong enough to make him "accept" Jesus if that is what he must do in order to find someone to be his friend. In this case he is not recognizing that he has a sin problem. He is not accepting Jesus as his Savior from sin, but is "accepting" Jesus as his guarantee of having as friends those who are presenting to him the gospel. He is not really saved, but his new friends probably think he is, and perhaps he will too.

No one is more subject to psychological pressure than a child. Whenever we discuss the gospel with a child, we must be sensitive to the tremendous pressures we are putting on him. We are not talking here about blatant forms of manipulation, such as offering prizes. We are talking about much more subtle forms of pressure. If we are his parents, simply telling him we want him to trust Jesus automatically applies a great deal of pressure because of his strong desire to please his parents. Even telling him that we have trusted in Jesus can exert a strong influence on him because of his identification with his parents and his desire to be like them.

Any adult can have a similar influence on children, so the problem is not limited to parents. So whatever our relationship is to the child, we need to be aware of how easily we as adults can manipulate him without even trying to. Whether the setting is a home, a camp, or a church meeting, beware of such practices as telling a child, "If you accept Jesus you will make me very happy," or offering a brand new Bible to everyone who comes forward to accept Jesus, or asking for all the children who want to accept Jesus to raise their hands (knowing that most children will peek to see what the other kids are doing).

Group pressure may often be even stronger than individual pressure. Sometimes we make the mistake of thinking that only teens are subject to the pressures of the group, but this is not the case. Children and adults are just as vulnerable to group influence. No one wants others to think that he is the odd one in the crowd.

But what about results? After all, the above practices appear to get the job done. However, it is only when we forget what our job in evangelism is that we would be satisfied with these kinds of results. The above practices *appear* to get results, but that is all. If we really understand the difference between a psychological conversion and a spiritual conversion, then we will see the danger of appearances. Remember that our job in evangelism is not to produce converts. That is God's work. Our responsibility is to make the gospel message as clear as possible, and in order to do so we must avoid all forms of pressure.

As a general rule we should talk with the person individually and get plenty of feedback from him in his own words. We should ask the Lord to help us to be sensitive to both the spiritual and the psychological dynamics that are occurring. Unfortunately, even the clearest presentation of the gospel may in some cases be clouded by strong psychological dynamics. While it is impossible to remove all interpersonal dynamics, it is certainly possible to become more and more sensitive to these dynamics and to avoid the pressures that block a person's understanding of the gospel.

PSYCHOLOGICAL CONVERSIONS CAUSED BY CONFUSION

If we want a person to understand sin and sin's consequences, *we should focus our discussion on sin itself and its immediate consequences* rather than on the daily problems the person is having. Often the secondary, psychological, and sociological results of sin are confused with the primary, spiritual results. These two different types of results of sin are differentiated in the chart below.

Jesus taught some things about the Holy Spirit which are of great help at this point. The Holy Spirit convicts the world of "guilt in regard to sin and righteousness and judgment" (John 16:8). Note that sin and righteousness and judgment relate to the left side of the chart below. This is where the Holy Spirit's conviction is focused, so this is where our discussion with the sinner should be focused.

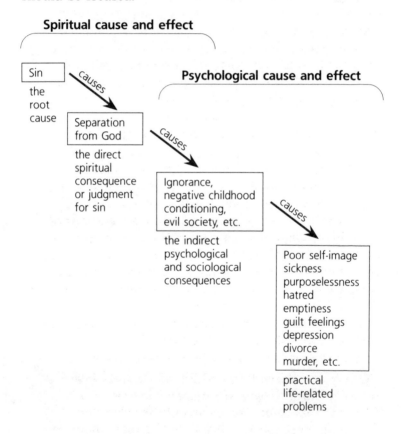

Spiritual cause and effect

Sin
the root cause

causes

Psychological cause and effect

Separation from God
the direct spiritual consequence or judgment for sin

causes

Ignorance, negative childhood conditioning, evil society, etc.
the indirect psychological and sociological consequences

causes

Poor self-image
sickness
purposelessness
hatred
emptiness
guilt feelings
depression
divorce
murder, etc.
practical life-related problems

Suppose you know a person who is an alcoholic. You might be tempted to tell him that Jesus is the answer to his alcoholism. Of course, it is true that when a person becomes a Christian, he then has the Holy Spirit within him to help him overcome all of his old patterns of living, including alcoholism. However, it is also true that the person may not connect his alcoholism with the underlying problem of sin. He may not see his alcoholism as a manifestation of sin, but merely as a weakness, or hindrance to a happier life. In other words, it is very easy for a person to want help for his problems, but never to deal with the underlying cause of those problems. In such a case, Jesus is not seen as "the Savior who died for my sin," but merely as the "savior" from a specific problem—not much different than the help he can get from Alcoholics Anonymous.

Help is available from a wide variety of sources for all sorts of problems. If a person's marriage is in trouble, he can get some help from a good marriage clinic. If gambling is ruining his life, group therapy might be able to help. If poor self-image, or depression, is the problem, friends or a good book or a trained counselor may help him achieve a better outlook on life.

Now, suppose we go to a person with one of these problems and discuss his need and then tell him that Jesus is the answer. We tell him he should accept Jesus as his Savior and his problem will be solved. In such a case he may "accept" Jesus, but for the wrong reason. He is viewing Jesus on the same level he would view the counselor, clinic, or therapy group. He may see Jesus as some sort of a mystical helper, but he probably does not see him as the holy Son of God who died to take the punishment for his sin. In fact, this person can go through the entire process of identifying and admitting his problem, and asking Jesus for help, yet he may never deal with his real spiritual problem, which is sin. Such a decision is a psychological decision but not a spiritual decision.

When specific life problems come into the discussion, we should try to help the person see the cause-effect relationships. He must come to grips with his underlying sin problem before he can see Jesus as his Savior in the biblical sense.

DANGERS

The most obvious danger resulting from a psychological conversion is that it gives the individual a false sense of hope. Since he has not truly received Jesus as his Savior from sin, he does not have the Holy Spirit residing within him to help him with his daily problems. In other words, even though he has "accepted" Jesus in order to get help with a certain problem, he is less likely to conquer that problem than he is if he had accepted Jesus as his Savior from sin and then had the Holy Spirit's direction and strength to cope with his daily difficulties.

Another danger with such a psychological conversion is that it hinders future evangelism. Such a person is not truly saved, yet he remembers "accepting" Jesus. Later someone else might go to him and talk with him about sin and Jesus and then tell him that he needs to accept Christ as his Savior. To this he is likely to reply, "I've already done that, and it didn't help much."

Whenever we focus a person's attention on a specific problem, we draw his attention away from the full gospel message. By focusing attention on a specific problem we are much more likely to present an incomplete gospel. On the other hand, when we use a specific problem to help the individual understand his underlying sin problem, we have begun to present the gospel properly.

FIVE
THE FAMILY,
THE HOME BASE
OF CHRISTIAN
MINISTRY

PRINCIPLE 17
The Place of the Family

PRINCIPLE 18
The Child's Nature and Needs

PRINCIPLE 19
Practical Guidance of the Child

THE PLACE
OF THE FAMILY

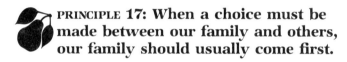 PRINCIPLE **17: When a choice must be made between our family and others, our family should usually come first.**

God has established three human agencies: the family, the church, and civil government. Each agency has its own special purpose, yet all three are interrelated. In this chapter we are concerned mainly with the family.

THE PARENT'S CHALLENGE

There are many reasons why families are important, but for now we will focus on just one reason—the ministry of the Christian family to its children.

A school-age child or teen is influenced from many sides during a typical week of his life. Each influence has its own unique impact in shaping the character and future of the individual. The numbers on the following diagram would vary greatly depending on the age of the child and the particular weekly pattern of the family.

Parents must realize that their share of influence on

their children, even though it begins at nearly 100 percent when the child is an infant, decreases year after year until the young adult leaves the family and the parents have little influence left. During most of the child's years, the parents are only one of several very strong influences. The challenge for the parents is obvious. They must make the most of the time they have to influence their children and teens. *They, not the church or some other Christian organization, are primarily responsible to evangelize their children and nurture them in the Lord* (Deut 6:6, 7; Eph. 6:1-4). But fulfilling this responsibility does not come easily. Commitment, prayer, planning, and hard work are required.

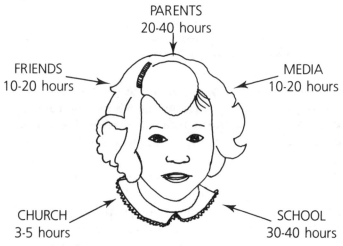

PARENTS
20-40 hours

FRIENDS
10-20 hours

MEDIA
10-20 hours

CHURCH
3-5 hours

SCHOOL
30-40 hours

THE PARENT'S PROBLEM

A Christian committed to Jesus Christ as Lord is also committed to the Bible as the Word of God. In turn, these commitments lead to something further— commitments to people—and here is where we face a problem. We cannot be equally committed to everyone.

Commitment requires a selection, a setting aside of many good concerns in order to devote ourselves to a few concerns. Of course, we are concerned about many people: the lost, maturing believers, neighbors, relatives, and our family. All of these concerns are good, but they raise many dilemmas. Should we attend the extra committee meeting or take that promised bike ride with our daughter? Should we join the evangelistic survey this afternoon or help our neighbor move his piano? Should we write a letter to an old friend tonight or talk with our wife or husband? At different times we should do all of these things, but at any given moment we must choose between one activity and another—that is, between one person and another.

REASONS FOR PUTTING OUR FAMILY FIRST

When a choice must be made between our family and others, our family should come first. The reasons are, first, a commitment to our family *already* exists. Marriage, rather than being the basis for a commitment, *is* a commitment. Even though as an adult we still have some obligations to our parents, our "family of birth" (1 Tim. 5:4), our commitment to our partner forms a "family of choice" which requires that we leave our parents in order to cleave to our partner (Gen. 2:24). We have already made a commitment to our family.

Second, we are called to our family just as much as we are called to Christian work. God calls us not merely to a certain full-time vocation or a certain location, but also to our family. The decision to marry and have children is no less a call than the decision to enter a particular ministry or move to a particular location. We are shortsighted if we quote Acts 20:32 and then skip off to our "calling."

Third, success with our family is one of God's requirements for leadership in the church or in a

Christian organization. "If anyone does not know how to manage his own family, how can he take care of God's church?" (1 Tim. 3:4, 5; see also Titus 1:6). Our family is our proving ground. If we neglect our family, we have sabotaged our other ministries.

Fourth, as parents we are more than providers. Provision for our family is important (1 Tim. 5:8), but much more is needed. We have not fulfilled our commitment to our family when we have merely paid for their shelter, food, clothing, insurance, and weekly allowance. Our example and instruction, which require our presence, are indispensable (Eph. 6:4).

Fifth, Christian agencies cannot take our place as parents. The church, Christian school, or Christian organization can supplement the ministry of our home but cannot replace it. Besides, the family is still the best setting for building character and purpose into our children's lives, as both Christian and non-Christian psychologists and educators recognize. A strong home contributes to both a strong church and a strong nation (Eph. 6:1-3).

ACTIONS

If we want our family to win, we might begin with these three steps: We must not take our family for granted. Second, we should find out the actual amount of time we are now devoting to our family. Third, each week we should do something with our family as a whole, and something with each member of our family individually.

We will frequently have to say "no" to others, but such choices are part of our commitment to our family.

THE CHILD'S NATURE AND NEEDS

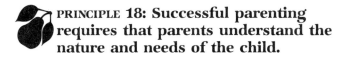 PRINCIPLE **18: Successful parenting requires that parents understand the nature and needs of the child.**

Many people are parents. Fewer people are successful parents. Producing a baby is one thing. Nurturing and guiding a child to become a self-directed and responsible young adult is another.

Christian parents need to draw upon all that their Christianity affords them to face the challenge of parenting. Prayer, guidance from Scripture, and the support of the church will all make a significant difference. However, our concern is not with the unique advantages that the Christian parent has, but with the basic psychological guidelines which apply to any home, Christian or not.

Unfortunately the word "discipline" has a very narrow meaning in many people's minds. To them it means only punishment. Some even view discipline so narrowly that they see it as opposed to love. But the Bible teaches that discipline is part of love (Heb. 12:6). Discipline properly understood includes both positive and negative instruction, example and demonstration, clear communication of expectations and consequences, rewards, and encouragement, as well as punishment. Neither one alone, the positive or the negative, is sufficient. The positive is needed to keep the child on the right path by making the path clear and attractive. The negative is needed to help the child return to the right path when he begins to step in a different direction. A parent who feels that the negative is sufficient will find his children attracted elsewhere. The parent who feels that the positive is sufficient is simply being unrealistic about the child's tendency to test the limits and go his own way.

In view of the narrow meaning often attached to the word "discipline," we will use a different phrase that is meant to emphasize both the positive and the negative: "practical guidance."

Since there is an overabundance of literature on this subject of the practical guidance of children in the home, our discussion here is quite abbreviated. This section and the next present ten key guidelines for parent-child relationships.

Parents should begin early to aim for responsible independence, emotional stability, and self-discipline. A child needs to grow, and he needs to grow up. Both of these processes are *gradual.* Being a grown-up includes responsible independence, emotional stability, and self-discipline, and parents need to begin encouraging these adult traits quite early. Some parents are satisfied with mere conformity as the goal. If their children obey them, they are pleased. But conformity to the parents' instructions is too shortsighted to be the legitimate goal of family nurture and practical guidance. Having a goal of conformity assumes that the child will always have a benevolent authority in charge of his behavior. Part of the parents' responsibility is to prepare their children to make their own decisions and their own contributions to society rather than merely following the directions of others all their lives.

Certainly obedience is expected, particularly from younger children. Children do need to learn to respect and respond to their parents' authority (Eph. 6:1; Col. 3:20). But parental authority does not last forever. Childhood in general, and adolescence in particular, are times of gradual transition to adult maturity. Parents who set their sights low and merely continue to demand obedience are not doing as much as they should to help the child learn to think for himself, make prudent decisions, and in general govern his own behavior and future, things which hasten the day when the parents can relate to their children as fellow adults and friends.

Each child is unique. Thus, the parents' approach to nurturing and guiding each child must also be unique. Even though two children have the same two parents and are brought up in the same house in the same general atmosphere, they will still have many differences. They may have different physical capabilities, different mental aptitudes, different energy levels, different needs for affection, different ways of showing affection, different hopes and aspirations, different needs for sleep, different levels of responsiveness, different strengths of will, different tastes and preferences, and many other differences.

Parents will not always be able to treat every child the same. Although consistency is important, no parent should be so consistent that he is insensitive to a child's unique needs and abilities. Telling one child he should be like another is definitely wrong. Being sensitive to each child's individual makeup and treating him accordingly is definitely all right.

Parents should do all they can to meet the organismic needs of their children. All children have inner drives, or organismic needs, which motivate their actions. Perhaps the most crucial needs for the parents to meet are those that are listed as social needs. The child needs to feel wanted and secure, to feel as though he has his own important place in the family, that others understand him and want to be with him. He should receive plenty of affection and love. And his actions should often be recognized, approved, and praised. Underlying all of these needs is the basic human need to feel worthwhile. Both through verbal means and through more subtle means the child should hear often that he is worthwhile.

Parents should cultivate a positive, yet realistic, self-image in their children. A child gains a picture of himself from his parents and friends, and from his actions. What others say about him, and how they respond to him, and his own assessment of his abilities and weaknesses come together to form his image of himself. This self-image, or self-concept, is cognitive—it is what he thinks he is like. His reaction to his self-image is his self-worth, or self-esteem—it is how important he thinks he is and how well he likes himself. Hardly anything is more crucial in governing moods, choices, and reaction patterns in the individual than his self-concept and his self-esteem.

A child needs assuring (but honest) feedback from adults and peers so that his resulting self-concept is positive, yet realistic. Of course, he will need to learn that he has sinned. But to be a sinner is not to be worthless, at least not in God's eyes, for "while we were still sinners, Christ died for us" (Rom. 5:8). So the basic theme of human self-worth does not need to be neglected, even during evangelism.

Children are imitators by nature. Parents need to exemplify what they want their children to imitate. "Monkey see, monkey do" is more than a witty phrase. It expresses a very significant truth which parents need to keep in mind. Children *will* imitate us and others, both our desirable and undesirable behavior. The child who sees or hears someone else's actions or speech either makes use of it soon or remembers it for use at an appropriate time. His senses are constantly looking for clues that will help him know how to behave in certain situations, as well as what behavior he can get away with. And the best type of clue is a real live demonstration by one of his parents.

This puts a heavy responsibility on parents in two ways. First, parents will find their children reflecting their own speech, behavior patterns, even facial expressions, gestures, and attitudes. At times parents will find this amusing; at other times it will bring them up short. But children probably learn more from their parents by imitation than by any other means.

If there are certain attitudes and values that we want our child to have, they must be consistently displayed year after year in our everyday contacts with the child. It is not enough merely to tell the child what values and attitudes to have. That is not the way values and attitudes are learned. He will *catch* our attitudes and values, even the ones we hope he doesn't notice.

Second, parents must be aware of who and what their children are observing, such as friends, literature, records, and television. A child who receives no guidance will imitate the level of the culture that surrounds him. The neglectful parent may then be shocked when he finds out how much his child learns through imitation. Parents have the opportunity, and the responsibility, to govern much of the input their children receive, and in turn this will significantly influence what they learn and how they live.

Parents must remember to accept their children as children and be patient with their normal immaturity. Even though all of us who are parents have very high hopes for our children, we must remember that being childish is acceptable during childhood. Obviously, this is a matter of degree. A six-year-old should not act like a two-year-old. It is all too easy for parents to forget what it was like to be a child and thus expect too much too soon. If we expect perfection from the child, he will develop a low self-image which can hamper his interpersonal relationships and achievements for the rest of his life.

This guideline must especially be applied in the emotional development of the child. Parents must consciously work at accepting their children's feelings, no matter how unreasonable those feelings might seem to the parents. Many parents unwittingly squelch communication with their children when they say, "You shouldn't feel that way." The fact is that he *does* feel that way. And when his parents don't accept those feelings as legitimate, the child knows that they don't understand him. He soon learns not to try to communicate his feelings to them, and the parent-child relationship takes a mechanical turn.

Parents need to help their children identify their feelings, then evaluate them, and finally govern those feelings. If feelings are denied, the child cannot even get started in this process. The more parents can learn to face and discuss their own feelings, the more they can help their children learn to do the same.

PRACTICAL GUIDANCE OF THE CHILD

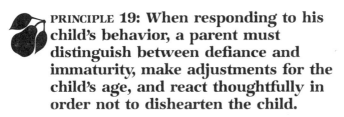 PRINCIPLE **19:** **When responding to his child's behavior, a parent must distinguish between defiance and immaturity, make adjustments for the child's age, and react thoughtfully in order not to dishearten the child.**

Parents should gradually adjust the strictness of their parenting style to the age of the child. Some parents feel that consistency means always expecting the same of their children and always reacting the same. However, a child needs a different parenting style when he is in preschool than when he is in high school. At a very young age a child should learn that his will is not the only one in the world, and that he is not the only person with desires and preferences. In particular, a young child needs to learn that his parents' will (that is, his parents' decision) often prevails over his own will. He needs to learn to accept this as a fact of life.

For the young child, a relatively strict parenting style is appropriate. A teenager, on the other hand, needs to have plenty of opportunity to make his own decisions, and even to make his own mistakes, which requires a considerable amount of freedom and encouragement from the parents. Some adolescent independence must be viewed as a good thing. If the adolescent does not learn to make his own choices and live with them, he will never become a genuine adult. During the middle childhood years, the parents should be making a gradual transition from the strictness of early childhood to the relative freedom of adolescence. A style which is firm, yet reasonable and flexible, is best. Thus, the parenting style is determined in part by the age of the child.

Parents frequently violate this guideline in three different ways. One way is to start strict and stay strict until the teen (who is still being treated as if he were a child) rebels in order to attain the independence that should have been gradually given to him. A second way is to begin too lenient, hoping to let the child express his own pleasant nature and reason with him when necessary. But young children do not reason the same way we do, and we soon find that his nature is not always as pleasant as we had hoped. And if we persist with our lenient approach we rob the child of something very important—that basic lesson of obedience which every child should learn very early in life. If he never learns to live with "No" when he is young, we can be sure that he will find it much more difficult to live with "No" when he gets older. This, by the way, is the meaning of Proverbs 22:6, "Train a child in the way he should go, and when he is old he will not turn from it."

Many have taken this verse as a promise to parents that, if trained properly from infancy, the child will live according to that training for the rest of his life. However, in the Hebrew this verse literally says, "Train up a child *according to his way*," and the most likely antecedent of "his" is "child." Thus, the point of the verse is that, if we try to train a child by letting him have his own way, when he is old he will always want to have his own way. (Compare Prov. 29:15.)

A third way in which parents violate the guideline is to attempt to become more strict after being lenient for a long time. Ideally, parents should begin relatively strict and gradually, over fifteen years or so, become more and more lenient and encourage more and more independence. But moving the other direction is much more difficult, if not impossible. If a parent realizes that he has made a mistake by being too lenient, he should not expect that he can suddenly demand total obedience as though his teen were suddenly a preschooler. That is a good way to bring disaster.

Parents must distinguish between defiance and immaturity and respond differently to each. If all we want is simplicity, we could say that all behavior can be divided into two types (from the parent's point of view), namely, desirable behavior and undesirable behavior. But if that is the only distinction we make as parents, we are sure to respond improperly to our child's actions much of the time. A further distinction is needed. Desirable behavior can be broken down into two categories: compliance and maturity. Undesirable behavior can also be broken down into two categories: defiance and immaturity.

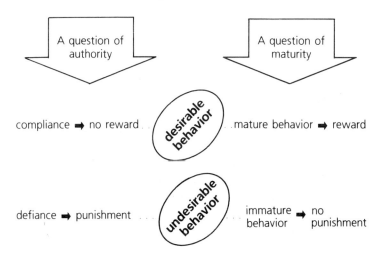

A question of authority

A question of maturity

compliance ➡ no reward   *desirable behavior*   mature behavior ➡ reward

defiance ➡ punishment   *undesirable behavior*   immature behavior ➡ no punishment

Defiant behavior is undesirable behavior in response to a clear directive or prohibition from the parent. In other words, when the parent clearly communicates to his child that he must not do a certain thing, but the child does it anyhow, that is defiance. However, when a child displays undesirable behavior which comes from his lack of experience and wisdom and his general immaturity, that is a different matter entirely. Defiant behavior takes place only when there is something to defy—some clear requirement or restriction from the parent. Other undesirable behavior is merely a matter of immaturity.

If parents keep these further distinctions in mind, they can respond appropriately to the various types of behavior. Mature behavior should be rewarded so that it is more likely to be repeated. But if we reward compliance, the child will learn to comply only for the reward. That is, he will have learned to bribe us so that he is obeying us because of the reward and not because of our legitimate authority. Similarly, defiance should be punished so that it is less likely to happen again. However, immature behavior should never be punished. It would be disheartening, indeed, for a child to be punished for acting his age.

Parental authority is easily abused. Parents must not dishearten their children. If we are exasperating or embittering our children, we are abusing our parental authority. "Do not exasperate your children" (Eph. 6:4). "Do not embitter your children" (Col. 3:21). These are commands addressed to parents. Some parents mistakenly feel that the Bible gives them the right to force their children to obey them, but there are no such commands directly addressed to parents. Instead, the commands about obedience are addressed to the children. If parents want to appeal to the Bible, then they should first be sure that they are doing what the Bible tells *them* to do. So, for parents the first question is not, "Are my kids obeying me?" Rather, the first question with which they should concern themselves is, "Am I disheartening my children?"

Parents exasperate and embitter their children in many different ways. One way is by having too many rules. Having just a few basic rules that are clearly communicated and consistently enforced usually works well. Another way to dishearten children is through inconsistency, which can show up in dozens of circumstances. One parent might not agree with the other. A parent's reactions might be governed by moods—harsh one day and understanding the next. One child might get favored treatment. The punishment might not be consistent with the disobedience. Promises and warnings might not be kept. Whenever it shows up, inconsistency confuses the child and makes it hard for him to learn anything but bitterness from the experience.

When parents are inconsistent and don't keep their word they destroy one of the most essential ingredients in family nurture and discipline: the child's confidence that his parents mean what they say.

The saying "Power corrupts" applies to parents as well as to politicians. When a parent exercises authority just to show who is boss, he is usually meeting his own ego needs rather than the needs of his child. If a child is ever going to learn to govern his own behavior, he needs to learn the reasons for certain choices or restrictions. Whenever these reasons can be understood by the child they should be explained to him. So when a child says "Why?" the parent should not respond with "Because I said so." Instead, the parent should explain his reasons (assuming he has good reasons to explain).

Punishment must be given thoughtfully, not merely as an emotional reaction. First we need to discuss whether or not physical punishment is even legitimate. Many psychologists and child experts feel that a parent should never use physical punishment on a child. They claim that any parent who strikes his child is exemplifying and encouraging violence. Their criticism of spanking and other forms of physical punishment is certainly justified in some cases. Suppose your preschooler has just clobbered a playmate with his sand bucket. You fly off the handle, spank him, and yell at him, "Don't you dare ever hit anyone again!" But the child is aware that *you* just hit someone, and it worked for you.

Does this obvious inconsistency mean that all forms of physical punishment should be forbidden? No, but it does mean that physical punishment can be easily misused. Punishment should never be given in a fit of anger. It should never be used to show who is boss, or to work off one's own frustrations.

Two ingredients make spanking different from violence. One is the parent's self-control (which is what parents are trying to develop in their children in the first place). The other is the proper motivation in using physical punishment. Some psychologists might still argue that even with self-control and proper motivation, parents who spank their kids are still modeling the sort of behavior they want to discourage. But when the parent is relatively calm, explains the reasons for the punishment, tells or shows the child what he should have done instead, and expresses his love for the child, the child can tell the difference.

Thus, parents must make every punishment a *thoughtful* punishment rather than a mere emotional outburst. One way to do this is to make sure that the punishment, whether it is physical or not, is appropriate to the "crime." Often you can allow the natural consequences of an action to serve as the punishment. A child who leaves a toy sitting outside overnight will have to put up with a rusty toy. His parents should not be too quick to replace it for him. But many times the natural consequences of an action do not come quickly enough or have enough impact by themselves. In such cases, parents must make sure that there are immediate and significant consequences so that the child "gets the message."

As a general rule, both rewards and punishments should follow an action quickly so that the child can make the connection in his own mind between the action and its consequence. Mothers should not say, "Wait until your father hears about this."

When parents have to add consequences because the natural consequences are not sufficient to teach the lesson, these added consequences should still be appropriate to the disobedience. For example, when a child steals some candy from the grocery store, what consequences should he face? Replacing the candy (or paying for it if he has already eaten it), or an apology to the store manager, or going without candy for a week, or all of these together would be appropriate to the crime and would afford opportunity to discuss the matter with the child. Other consequences that are less appropriate to the disobedience, and therefore less helpful in correcting the behavior, include such old time favorites as a hasty spanking, sending the child to his room, or withholding some unrelated privilege.

While disobedience should be followed by punishment, other things should also follow disobedience. In order for the punishment to have its best effect, it should be combined with such things as correction, instruction, example, and encouragement. The parent's task is not over when the punishment has been given. Remember that discipline is practical guidance—it is positive as well as negative. Punishment should seldom be the only response of the parents. If parents view themselves as practical guides for their children rather than as resident policemen, they will include both the positive and the negative.

SIX
DISCIPLE MAKING, THE PERSONAL STRATEGY OF CHRISTIAN MINISTRY

PRINCIPLE 20
Disciple Making Described

PRINCIPLE 21
Following Jesus' Example

DISCIPLE MAKING DESCRIBED

 PRINCIPLE **20: Disciple making is a deliberate and extended ministry of personal guidance aimed at developing Christian reproducers.**

WHAT IS DISCIPLE MAKING?

The words "disciple making," "discipling," and "discipleship" are often used to refer to the same idea. But since "discipling" is occasionally confused with "discipline," and since "discipleship" for a long time was used to refer to individual dedication, the word "disciple making" is used here.

Some writers limit disciple making to the period that precedes salvation; that is, they equate disciple making with evangelism. Other writers limit disciple making to the period that follows salvation; that is, they equate disciple making with edification. However, the great commission in Matthew 28:18-20 covers both periods. It refers to making disciples among nations which do not yet know Jesus (evangelism). Also, as part of the disciple making process, it refers to teaching individuals to observe all of Jesus' commands (edification).

Here is a definition of disciple making which includes both evangelism and edification: Disciple making is a deliberate process in which one older Christian deals *personally* with one or more other people over an extended period of time, *guiding* their experiences so that they ultimately develop into Christians who are mature and able to do the same with still others.

A DELIBERATE PROCESS

The definition states that disciple making is a deliberate process. In contrast to the spontaneous evangelism and nurture which occur now and then as unexpected opportunities arise, disciple making is planned. There are two basic kinds of activities which the older Christian might plan for one or several younger Christians. The first kind involves regular meetings, perhaps once each week at a regular time and place. Everyone knows what Bible passages will be studied or what topic will be discussed. Of course, there is plenty of room for open discussion of any issue that comes up, and the atmosphere is very informal. Yet these meetings are more planned than the second kind of activity in the sense that the lessons that arise are more predictable.

The second kind of activity is planned only in the sense that some general, real-life experience is initiated by the older Christian. The particular lessons that will arise during these experiences are not precisely known ahead of time. For example, suppose a Christian who is experienced in door-to-door evangelism takes a new Christian with him. The older Christian does not know precisely what reception they will receive at each home, what the religious backgrounds of the people will be, or what specific questions or objections they might face. So in that sense these experiences are spontaneous. Yet, they are "planned" in the sense that none of these experiences would occur and no lessons would be learned if the visitation had not been initiated by the older Christian.

Thus, disciple making is deliberate; that is, it is planned. And both kinds of planned activities are needed—regular meetings, and real-life experiences.

AN EXTENDED PROCESS

The definition also states that disciple making occurs over an extended period of time. It is not merely two visits to a new believer's home, or one long counseling session. Disciple making is more likely to take years. The profoundly personal nature of disciple making requires that bonds of trust and intimacy be established. This requires many months. Also, an extended period of time is required simply because (1) the Bible is such a large book, (2) there are so many questions to be answered, (3) so many skills to learn, and (4) such a wide variety of things to experience.

Our culture discourages lengthy involvements both because families move from town to town so frequently and because everyone seems to have such a busy schedule. If disciple making is to happen at all, it must be given a high priority and other endeavors may have to be sacrificed. Making disciples requires a high level of commitment.

A PROCESS OF GUIDING

The definition also refers to disciple making as a process of guiding. Disciple making is not indoctrination. The disciple maker guides others through experiences which will help them understand the Bible and its teachings better, and will help them live the Christian life more consistently and effectively.

A mature Christian is a thinking person. He understands the Christian faith. He is able to discern the

Lord's direction for his life from the principles in Scripture and from the leading of the Holy Spirit. He is *not* a carbon copy of his discipler. He is *not* a well-programmed computer, full of canned answers. Rather, he is himself—a follower of Jesus, not a follower of any human being.

Thus, it is not good for the disciple maker to think of those with whom he works as "his" disciples. Their task is not to learn to follow him. Of course, his example is extremely crucial. Nevertheless, Jesus' example is more crucial. When we make disciples, our basic invitation is not "Come follow me," but "Come follow Jesus with me." We must watch out for the subtle temptation to enjoy disciple making because we enjoy having followers. Instead, we should engage in disciple making because we enjoy following Jesus and want others to follow him too. Throughout history there have been "disciple makers" who have not guided, but have captivated followers and even turned them into mindless worshipers of the "discipler." When we disciple others, we do not dominate them—we *liberate* them!

A CYCLIC PROCESS

The definition describes the end result of disciple making as the production of reproducers, which is a very long-range goal. It is more than assurance of salvation, more than increased Bible knowledge, more than victory over temptation, more than the ability to lead others to Christ. It is the ability to reproduce others who can also reproduce others.

Certainly Paul saw his disciple Timothy as one who would reproduce other reproducers. In fact, in his instructions to Timothy, Paul spoke of several cycles: the Paul-Timothy cycle, the Timothy-reliable men cycle, and the reliable men-others cycle (2 Tim. 2:2). While we cannot actually see several generations ahead, we *can* think of the person we are discipling as a future disciple maker himself.

One other aspect of the definition—perhaps the most significant—is that disciple making is profoundly personal. This aspect of disciple making is so important that the entire next principle is devoted to it.

DISCIPLE MAKING IS IDEAL FOR CHANGING VALUES

Values are deep seated in the individual and they are not easily changed. They are "caught" through subtle interpersonal processes. A simple lecture, no matter how skillfully organized or presented, can seldom alter values.

However, the processes that take place in disciple making are nearly ideal for changing values. Mutual *respect* and *rapport* grow between discipler and disciple. The disciple observes a consistent *example* over a long period of time. The discipler can raise *guiding questions* during unhurried discussions. And when small peer groups are involved these influences can be especially strong. Next to parenting, disciple making is the best means of affecting an individual's value system.

DISCIPLE MAKING AND OUR TRADITIONAL MINISTRIES

Disciple making is not something that is distinct from such traditional fields as Christian education, the pastorate, and missions. Instead, disciple making is the core which all of these ministries have in common. The Christian educator, the pastor, and the missionary are all disciple makers.

Of course, each of these traditional ministries has a unique emphasis. The missionary usually does his disciple making in a location or in a culture different from his own. The pastor focuses most of his disciple making on those who are already saved and in one local congregation. The Christian educator (this, by the way, is the hardest of the three to nail down because of the breadth of the field of Christian education) carries out his disciple making with special sensitivity to the nature of the learner and the educational process.

Distinct emphases could also be cited for many more Christian workers, including evangelists, counselors, publishers, radio and television broadcasters, and even parents. But basically they are all doing the same thing—making disciples. Whatever our profession, whether it is one of the traditional Christian ministries or not, we should see ourselves as disciple makers. Disciple making is not merely the responsibility of the pastors and leaders of the church; it is the responsibility of the whole church.

Many people never get involved as disciple makers because they feel that there is no one around for them to disciple. If we have children we have someone to disciple. If we have neighbors we can begin contacting and evangelizing them. If we are a church member we probably have even more people whom we could help. The real issue is not a lack of people needing guidance, but a lack of courage and time. Both of these lacks can be overcome by the person who really *wants* to be a disciple maker.

141

FOLLOWING
JESUS' EXAMPLE

 PRINCIPLE **21: Our ministries must follow
Jesus' example, which was profoundly
personal.**

Jesus ministered occasionally to large crowds, often to
individuals, and to various sized groups in between
these two extremes.

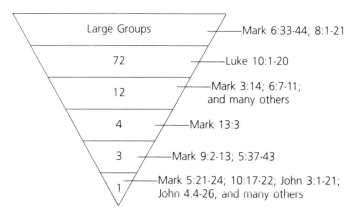

Although Jesus ministered to all sizes of groups, he
concentrated his ministry on individuals and his band of

twelve followers. Our balance should probably be the same. We must never neglect the masses, yet we must spend a large share of our time with individuals and small groups. The larger the group we are working with, the shallower the interaction. The smaller the group, the deeper the interaction. When we are talking with one person we can get to know him better and deal with his concerns much more directly than we can when he is part of a large group.

We will do well to study and emulate Jesus' ministry—the supreme example and standard for all Christian workers. We will examine here only a few incidents from the Gospels to illustrate the personal nature of Jesus' ministry.

EATING

Jesus ate with people, both sinners and saints (Mark 2:15). Eating with someone is very personal, and a very good way to get to know someone. Often we will be in his home or he will be in ours. The atmosphere will be (hopefully) informal. We will have plenty of time for conversation, which can proceed at a comfortable pace because we are doing other things as well as talking.

The fact that Jesus ate with others is especially remarkable. After all, Jesus did not have to eat with anyone. He certainly did not need anyone else's food, for he could instantly produce all the food he wanted. He must have done it simply because it was the best way to minister—the personal way.

AFTER CLASS

We find repeatedly throughout the Gospels that Jesus was available "after class" (Mark 4:10). Sometimes teachers make the mistake of thinking that their ministry takes place during class and that is the end of it. After class they run to get their choir robes on and hurry through the song one last time.

But it is often after class that the conversations turn personal. When a class member makes the extra effort to stay after class to ask a question, the teacher can be sure that it is important to him. Also, the mere fact that he asks it after class instead of during class may be a clue that it is highly personal. Often out-of-class contacts with students have more impact than the in-class contacts.

This is not meant to minimize the class time, because the questions that are asked after class are often created by the class discussion. On the other hand, as students get to know teachers better and respect them because of out-of-class contact, the in-class statements will have more integrity in students' eyes, and therefore more impact. Thus, while class time is important, the in-class contact and the out-of-class contact work best in combination. Each one contributes to the other. The out-of-class contact adds the personal dimension that the in-class contact needs in order to be most effective.

Again, it is remarkable that Jesus took so much time with what we would call slow learners. Since he was the Son of God and spoke with complete authority, he might have simply appeared, stated the truth once, and then returned to seclusion. But Jesus was not just interested in stating the truth. He was also concerned for people and their need to grasp the truth.

TRAVELING

Jesus traveled with his disciples (Mark 4:35-41). Interesting things often happen when people travel, and the storm that arose on this boat trip must have been one of the disciples' most interesting experiences with Jesus prior to his resurrection. This was not only a real-life experience, it was a life-and-death occasion. One of

Jesus' tasks early in his ministry was to establish his identity in the minds of his followers. This demonstration of his power to calm a furious storm effectively established the idea that he was no ordinary man.

What if Jesus had merely stood in the synagogue and claimed to be the divine Son of God with power over the forces of nature. Who would have believed him? That sort of claim had to be demonstrated. What an effective demonstration it was! And with what intense pupil involvement! We can be sure the disciples were not yawning during this lesson. With their own eyes they saw him stop the wind and the waves, so any claim to deity that he might make later would carry undeniable weight.

Our task as teachers and disciple makers is actually quite similar to Jesus' task. We also make a claim to have divine power. And our claim, no less than Jesus' claim, must be demonstrated in real life in order to command belief. While we can't stop storms, we claim to have divine help to overcome temptation, divine wisdom to make prudent decisions, divine comfort in times of sorrow, a divine source of patience and self-control in frustrating circumstances, and many other superhuman advantages. If we merely talk about our divine source of power, who will believe us? But if we live, work, and travel with people where they can see God's power in action, our talk will mean much more. The more we *show* our Christianity, the more we have the right to *speak* our Christianity. And the best place to demonstrate our Christianity is in those activities and places where others are already personally involved.

A WAY OF LIFE

The above incidents are only a few of many that could be cited. Over and over again Jesus ministered in a personal manner. It was his way of life. He hand picked a small group to witness his transfiguration (Mark 9:2). After he rose from the dead he appeared personally to Peter and later to James, even though both of these men were present to witness his resurrection twice when he appeared to the twelve apostles (1 Cor. 15:5-7). He even made a special appearance to Thomas to give him the evidence he needed in order to be convinced of the resurrection (John 20:24-29). Shortly before Jesus' ascension to heaven he helped his disciples catch fish, and prepared a breakfast for them (John 21:5-12). Personal ministry is best seen not as an occasional extra which is added to our usual ministry, but as a continuous way of life.

SENSITIVITY TO NEEDS

One day Jesus actually walked away from a crowd in order to minister personally to Jairus and his daughter (Mark 5:21-24). We often mistakenly feel that the more who hear us at once, the greater impact we are having. This incident is remarkable because it shows Jesus on this occasion choosing a ministry to a few *over* a ministry to many.

Yet it would be unfair to claim that this was always Jesus' preference, for just the opposite also occurred. Once when Jesus left a crowd in order to be alone with his disciples, the crowd followed them, and then Jesus turned to the crowd because of his compassion on them (Mark 6:30-34). Evidently, there is no hard and fast rule which says "Fewer is always better than many." If that were the rule, Jesus would have ignored the crowd in this last incident. While it is true that Jesus ministered to individuals and to small groups most often, he was never insensitive to the needs of the masses.

It is not the size of the group which determines which one we minister to, but the *needs* of the group, and how those needs can be best met. Usually, but not always, the needs can be satisfied best individually or in small groups rather than in large groups.

PURPOSELY PERSONAL

Jesus' ministry was, through and through, a personal ministry. And this was no accident. Right from the beginning, when the twelve apostles were appointed, Jesus' plan was "that they might be with him" (Mark 3:14). This was no long-distance instruction; it was personal by design. Later, Jesus gave his "great commission" to these disciples. He told them to "Go and make disciples of all nations . . . teaching them to observe everything I have commanded you" (Matt. 28:19, 20). No doubt they remembered their own personal experiences with Jesus and knew exactly what he had in mind. In essence, Jesus told his disciples to do with others what he had been doing with them.

The great commission which Jesus gave his disciples is actually a command to *guide* individuals to become believers and grow toward reproductive Christian maturity. We notice that the command sets up a repeating cycle so that the command is given anew to each successive generation of Christians. Thus, in a very real sense, Jesus tells *us* to make disciples—to guide others personally as he himself did.

HOW PAUL MINISTERED

After Paul evangelized the Thessalonians and established a church there, his ministry came under heavy attack from the jealous Jews in the region. When Paul wrote a letter to the Thessalonians, he found it necessary to remind them how he ministered to them so that the accusations of the jealous Jews would not spoil the impact of his ministry. Notice the personal nature of Paul's ministry from his own description. "We were gentle among you, like a mother caring for her little children. We loved you so much that we were delighted to share with you not only the gospel of God but our lives as well, because you had become so dear to us. . . . We dealt with each of you as a father deals with his own children" (1 Thess. 2:7-11).

OUR CHALLENGE

For three years Jesus concentrated his efforts on a small group of men. Rather than doing a shallow work in many, he did a deep and lasting work in a few, so that these few were able to lead the next generation. In approximately 350 years Christianity had spread so much that it became the primary religion of the Roman empire. But what has happened since then? Institutionalization with its deadening emphasis on programs and agencies (rather than on people) has caused the church to lose ground ever since. It is about time we begin to pay attention to Jesus' example.

Our present pattern is to increase the church by addition, a few mature Christians winning many others. The scriptural pattern is to increase the church by multiplication, every mature Christian discipling a few others so that in time there are many mature Christians, each able to reproduce himself in the lives of others. We may be tempted to think that we have found something better with our vast organizations, mass communication, and high technology. This is why we, perhaps more than any previous generation, need to be reminded that our ministries must follow Jesus' example, which was profoundly personal.

A CONTRAST

Perhaps we can get a better picture of how far we are from Jesus' example if we compare the features of a typical structured program with the features of disciple

making. Each point of contrast in the chart below is
self-explanatory.

	STRUCTURED PROGRAM	DISCIPLE MAKING
1. Time	One shot, or weekly, or monthly	Extended and continual
2. Number	Usually many	Few
3. Selectivity	Everyone is welcome	Hand-picked
4. Depth	Shallow	Intimate
5. Intentionality	Planned in detail	Planned and spontaneous
6. Leader relationship	Contact is indirect (One interacts with programs more than with persons)	Contact is direct
7. Feedback	Little	Much
8. Curriculum (experiences)	Geared to average needs	Geared to individual needs
9. Connotation	"Our program will go on without you"	"You are important"
10. Summary	IMPERSONAL	PERSONAL

Some would unwisely conclude that we ought to do
away with all of our structured programs,
organizations, and agencies. First, we should do
everything possible to make our programs more
personal, direct, individualized, and spontaneous.
Second, we should make sure that we are not relying
solely on the program or the organization, but are
taking steps ourselves to disciple a few individuals.

STEPS TO TAKE
Jesus' pattern of disciple making can be boiled down to
three basic steps: (1) selection, (2) instruction, and
(3) apprenticeship.

Selection is hard to do. Our culture teaches us to be
democratic and treat everyone equally. However, not
everyone has the same needs. Nor does everyone have
the same level of readiness to learn. If we are going to
do any disciple making at all, we must select a few and
concentrate our efforts on these. This was Paul's
command to his disciple, Timothy. "The things you

have heard me say . . . entrust to reliable men who will also be qualified to teach others" (2 Tim. 2:2). Paul advised Timothy not to try to teach everyone himself. Rather, he was to select those who could multiply his teaching ministry.

Instruction, or teaching, is carried on both verbally and nonverbally. Once we have selected one or a few individuals to disciple, we must personally discuss biblical truths with them *and* personally demonstrate how those truths work out in our life and ministry. Discussion without demonstration is too theoretical. Demonstration without discussion loses much of its precision and is easily misinterpreted. Both discussion and demonstration require planning, as described in the previous section. If we plan both regular meetings and real-life experiences, we will have plenty of opportunity for both discussion and demonstration.

Apprenticeship is personally supervised practice. No single schedule of assignments can be devised for all people. Instead, learning opportunities must be personally devised so that they include plenty of success experiences, and so that they require progressively more maturity and skill. Apprenticeship should be thought of not so much as a testing device but as a teaching device. Such an apprenticeship should lead the individual to have confidence that the Lord can work through him to minister to others.

These three steps are, of course, an oversimplification of the process. Once the process of disciple making is started, the Lord gives direction regarding the details. Our problem, however, is not that the process gets started and then fails because we don't know exactly what to do next. Our problem is that we never get started, we never select.

SEVEN
TEACHING, AN ESSENTIAL INGREDIENT OF CHRISTIAN MINISTRY

TEACHING: WELL-AIMED GUIDANCE

 PRINCIPLE 22: Teaching is guiding people through learning experiences which are carefully aimed to meet specific needs in their lives.

"In your teaching show integrity, seriousness, and soundness of speech" (Titus 2:7, 8).

TEACHING IS GUIDING

Teaching includes many things: demonstrating, sharing, motivating, helping learners discover, listening, correcting, being an example, lecturing, discussing, and much more. An extremely narrow view of teaching might equate it with giving a well-planned lecture to a classroom full of students sitting in straight rows. But a healthy view of teaching is rich and broad.

Perhaps the best synonym for the word "teaching" is the word "guiding," because guiding can be done in any setting and in almost any way. When we think of teaching as guiding we are also reminded of two things that are crucial in good teaching. We are reminded that learners are being guided *toward* something and that the learners themselves must be *personally involved* and moving toward the goal. These two things, better known as aims and meaningful student involvement, are absolutely essential if the teaching is going to be effective.

Aims are discussed in this section; meaningful learner involvement is discussed with Principle No. 25.

THE LECTURE HANG-UP

Some people feel that when they are teaching the Bible they should lecture because of the authority of the Bible. They argue that, since the Bible is the inspired, reliable, authoritative Word of God, the only method which reflects properly on the nature of the Bible is an authoritative method—lecturing. Since the teacher already has the truth, he does not need to ask questions, listen to student opinions, or hold discussions.

But if we notice how Jesus taught, we will quickly set this bogus viewpoint aside. Throughout his teaching ministry Jesus involved his followers in the learning process. Although he lectured at times, he often asked questions and encouraged discussion.

There are several reasons why a Bible teacher should encourage his students to raise questions, express various viewpoints, and thoroughly discuss the lesson. First, a learner who is sitting quietly *might* be thinking about the lesson, or he might not be. But a learner who is asking questions or expressing his ideas certainly has his mind on the lesson. Second, when the teacher is responsive to the learners' questions and comments, the lesson will automatically be more relevant to the learner. Third, encouraging the learner to speak up indicates to him that the teacher values his thoughts and ideas (and by implication, values him), which helps build acceptance and rapport between teacher and learner. Fourth, hearing from the learner allows the teacher to discover more of the learner's background and how much knowledge he brings to each subject. And fifth, encouraging the learner to respond with comments and questions supplies the teacher with feedback about the lesson at hand, which helps the teacher know whether or not he is communicating his ideas effectively.

INGREDIENTS FOR EFFECTIVE GUIDING

Several ingredients go into being an effective guide. First, we must desire to minister to others. Our learners should get the idea that we like teaching, and that one of the best things about teaching is that we get to be with them and talk with them. In other words, we are enthusiastic about being a Christian and about helping others enjoy the Christian life too. However, this desire to teach should be more than just a desire to do something that we enjoy. It also should reflect a spiritual motivation which grows out of the seriousness and urgency of teaching.

Second, we must be dedicated and faithful to our learners. Dedication to *learners* is probably a more healthy concept than dedication to *teaching*. This dedication will show up in the amount of out-of-class contact we have with each individual and the quality of preparation that goes into each lesson.

Third, we must practice what we teach. Our consistent example is a live demonstration that our verbal lessons will work. Our learners will gain confidence both in us as a person and in what we say because of what they observe in our life.

Fourth, we must know what we are talking about.

Our Bible knowledge should constantly be increasing. So should our grasp of systematic theology. So should our ability to integrate theology with other fields such as psychology, literature, history, or science.

Fifth, we must pray and rely on the work of the Holy Spirit. Remember that we are teaching lessons that go against the sinful nature and are thus supernatural. Such lessons cannot be learned without the aid of the Holy Spirit. He will always be "on the job," but our responsibility is to remember our dependence on him. In prayer we can talk to the Lord about each individual learner and about the supernatural lessons we hope he will learn under our guidance.

Sixth, we must be sensitive to our learner's needs, interests, and fears. We must constantly build mutual respect, rapport, and friendship between us and our learners. Only as we are sensitive to their needs will our lessons be relevant to them.

Seventh, we must develop our teaching skills. We should feel comfortable leading a group in discussion and using a variety of other teaching methods.

Eighth, we must be patient both with ourselves and with our learners.

AIMS BASED ON NEEDS

A teacher is a guide, and a guide always has a destination in mind. This is where aims come into the picture. An aim can be defined simply as a statement of intended result. Of course, the long-range goal is complete Christian maturity. But the teacher should also have subgoals or short-range aims in mind which will bring about a steady movement toward the long-range goal. These might be aims for the year, or the quarter, or the individual lesson. In the remainder of this section we will focus on the aims that are written for single lessons.

All lessons are based on aims and all aims are based on needs, as indicated in the diagram below.

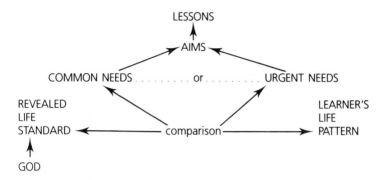

Ultimately teaching and learning all go back to God and his nature. Because God is holy, he has revealed a life standard for human beings that reflects his own holy nature. But the learner's present pattern of life is far from God's standard. By comparing the learner's life pattern with the revealed life standard we come up with the learner's needs. These needs are often common needs, that is, the typical needs we would expect a person of a given age to have.

The writers of curriculum materials are well aware of these common needs and they gear their lessons to meet them. But the learner's needs may be urgent needs, that is, needs which are unique to our group of learners at any given moment. Other groups the same age as our learners may not have these needs, and our group may not have these same needs in two more months. Aims are then written based on one of the common needs or on an urgent need.

Finally, the lesson is planned and taught according to the aim that has been written. If lessons are not based on aims and if aims are not based on needs, it is all too easy for the teacher to teach irrelevant lessons—lessons *he* likes but which are of little value to his learners.

BALANCING COMMON NEEDS AND URGENT NEEDS

Some say we should teach what the class is interested in learning. Others say we should stick with the lessons printed in the curriculum materials. We can maintain a healthy balance if we keep two words in mind: motivation and framework.

First, motivation is crucial. Without motivation our "learners" will learn little or nothing. When they express an urgent need, ask an important question, or show that they are troubled by some current issue, we can be sure that they are at the edge of learning and are motivated. We should never throw motivation away. When we find it, we must use it, by going with the interest of the hour so that our lesson will be relevant and students will learn.

Second, a framework is crucial. If we are always gearing our lessons to the hot topics of the day, our learners may never establish a biblical or theological framework. They need to become familiar with the content of each book of the Bible and with the general flow of both Old and New Testament history. They need to work toward the goal of being able to picture in their minds a timeline with key persons and key events in their proper places. They should become more and more familiar with the various areas of theology so that they can relate any current topic to the general outline of biblical doctrine. Working toward the development of such a framework eventually will help them answer their own urgent questions because they will know where to go in the Bible and what theological issues to bring into the discussion.

We should combine the advantage of motivation with the advantage of the framework. On the one hand, when an urgent problem arises, we should deal with it explicitly, but not stop there. We should go on to show how that problem relates to more basic theological issues and how the key Scripture passages used in discussing the problem relate to their larger context and to the general flow of the book of the Bible in which they are found. In this way we can help the learners develop their framework while we are discussing an urgent problem. On the other hand, when we are surveying a Bible book or discussing a basic doctrine, we need to establish connections with current issues and questions that will interest our learners. In this way we can help them gain an interest in the "framework" and begin to see its relevance to their lives.

DISCOVERING THE LEARNERS' NEEDS

Needs, especially urgent needs, are only discovered as we become familiar with our learners' current life patterns. This requires a lot of time spent with them, preferably on their turf. We cannot get to know people very well during class time. The more we can observe each individual in informal settings, and talk with him about his interests in a nonthreatening atmosphere, the more we will get to know what he is really like. Only then can we teach "what is helpful for building others up according to their needs" (Eph. 4:29).

A notebook is helpful to keep our information on each learner organized and handy. For each person in our class we might have one page for information that is fairly stable (such as name, age, address, phone number, names of family members, date of conversion, talents, hobbies, positions in the church, etc.) and another page for a list of strengths and weaknesses. As we prepare each lesson we can review the strengths and weaknesses of each person in the class and in this way be sure that our aims are based on their needs. If we are truly teaching lessons that are geared to our learners' needs, we should occasionally be able to scratch out some of the things we have recorded as weaknesses and add some strengths.

TWO KINDS OF AIMS

As we write aims for our learners, some of them should be knowledge aims and some should be action aims. Dealing with the type of biblical or doctrinal information that our learners should store for future recall and use calls for a *knowledge aim*. Dealing with the type of information that our learners should apply in their daily lives without delay calls for an *action aim*.

Everything we teach should be usable. It may be used mentally to support certain beliefs or to add perspective to our outlook. Or, it may be used to share with a friend. Or, it may be used to help make practical decisions, that is, applied in our daily life. But not everything we teach should be used immediately. Some of this practical information should be stored for future use when the time is appropriate. Thus, the way we determine whether a lesson should have a knowledge aim or an action aim is not to ask whether the information is useable. Rather, we should ask when this information should be used. If it should be used immediately to make a change in our daily life pattern, then the lesson should have an action aim. If it should be stored and recalled later when the situation calls for this information, then the lesson should have a knowledge aim. Here are some sample aims.

Knowledge Aims

To become familiar with the New Testament qualifications for the pastor (elder)

To understand nonbiblical explanations of Christ's death, and why they are false

To see how the doctrine of salvation requires the doctrine of the Trinity

To appreciate the accuracy of certain Old Testament prophecies

Action Aims

To maintain a regular personal Bible study program

To pray daily for our civil leaders

To seek out discouraged believers and encourage them

To worship the Lord privately every day

To be more understanding and patient with fellow workers

We divide aims into these two types because of our analysis of the functions of the inner person, as explained under Principle 5. Obviously, the knowledge aim relates to the intellect and the action aim relates to the volition and the resultant actions. Some have suggested that we also ought to have affective (or feeling, or inspirational) aims, which would relate to the emotions.

Naturally, if you are dealing with an action aim, then it is legitimate also to have a knowledge aim and an affective aim that are prerequisites to the action. In such a case the threefold aim would spell out what the person should know, how he should feel, and what he should do. Affective aims that are part of a unified package are legitimate, but affective aims should not be used by themselves. The reason will be obvious to us if we recall how the emotions differ from the intellect. Knowledge can be stored without frustrating the person, so it is often appropriate to stop there. But emotions are not stored. If we give a person information that stirs him up emotionally so that he has strong feelings or desires, we should also give him a means of expressing those feelings or desires. In other words, those strong emotions should be followed by a decision and an action. To stir up emotions as an end in itself is to frustrate the normal pattern of internal functions.

There is only one legitimate stopping place along the sequence of inner functions—the intellect. And thus there are only two legitimate types of aims, knowledge aims and action aims.

WRITING AND USING AIMS

If an aim is going to be of any practical help to us as a teacher, we need to have our aim carefully worded and at the front of our conscious thinking while we are preparing the lesson. For this reason it is wise to write out our aim for each lesson and keep it in sight.

We have already emphasized that our aim must be based on learner needs, and that some of our aims should be knowledge aims while others should be action aims. A good aim, first, should be worded in terms of the learner. It should state the intended result for the learner rather than the activity of the teacher. For example, the aim, "to *present* the New Testament qualifications of the pastor" tells what the teacher will do, not what the result will be for the learner. Watch out for aims that begin with words "to show," "to explain," or "to give."

Second, our aim should be brief, perhaps twelve words or less. Shorter aims are easier to work with and easier to remember.

Third, the aim should be singular, aimed at one thing. If we try to achieve several goals in one lesson we are less likely to get anything accomplished than if we had aimed at only one thing.

Fourth, our aim should be specific. General aims like the following will not do much to help the students apply the lesson in daily life: "to love everybody," "to pray about everything," "always to make the right decisions." If we aim at something general, we will probably end up with learners who are merely able to state generalizations. But if we aim at something specific, we are more likely to end up with learners who act.

Fifth, our aim should be achievable. Take things one step at a time. Remember, we want our learners to have a string of success experiences, so we must put the goal within reach.

But beautiful aims are no good unless we *use* them in our teaching. Before the lesson, we should think of the aim as we pray about each student by name. We should think of it as we gather materials and illustrations for the lesson, and when we sit down to plan the steps of the lesson. During the lesson, we should use it to help us decide whether to pursue a tangent question or to stay on the track. We might think of it as we lead the class in a discussion of their application of the lesson. After class, we could use the aim (if it is an action aim) to remind ourselves to contact our learners and encourage practical carry-over and application. And, of course, we could use the aim to evaluate the lesson. The main question we should use to evaluate our lesson is whether or not the aim was accomplished. (This, by the way, is one of the reasons for wording the aim in terms of the learner. If we word the aim in terms of our own activity as the teacher, then we may be able to claim that the aim was accomplished, but that will not say anything about the results for the learners. If it is worded in terms of the learners, it becomes a much more valid basis for evaluation.)

LEARNER ORIENTED TEACHING

 PRINCIPLE 23: Teachers should think in terms of the learner. Teaching should be graded to learner's vocabulary, age characteristics, and needs, and should be encoded according to his field of experience.

DO WE TEACH LESSONS OR LEARNERS?

Teaching involves three basic ingredients: the learner, the teacher, and the curriculum or content of the lesson to be learned. Some modern teachers have claimed that only two of these ingredients are important. They view teaching as merely teaching learners, and thus they neglect the importance of the content. The modern philosophy from which this viewpoint stems overemphasizes the importance of the process or the experience and discards the content and the goal. This philosophy values the journey but has nowhere to go. Any approach to teaching which neglects the importance of the content is just as meaningless.

But the opposite error is just as bad. Some teachers, instead of discarding the content, actually discard the learner. They think of teaching as merely teaching lessons. Of course, they are aware of the presence of the learner, but they feel that the content and its orderly presentation are the important things and thus give little or no consideration to the vocabulary, age, needs, and background of the learner. The result is that they have meaningful content to share, but it never becomes meaningful to the learner.

Obviously, we need to have a balanced view of teaching which recognizes the importance of both the learner and the lesson. We need to think of teaching as *teaching learners lessons.*

We have already stressed the importance of content by pointing out that the Bible's teachings are an essential part of a truly Christian ministry, and by thoroughly discussing the content of the gospel message. The error that creeps into evangelical churches most often is the error of glorifying the content and neglecting the learner. So, in this section we will focus our attention on the learner and the various ways we should gear our teaching and our communication to him so that we will be genuinely teaching *learners* lessons.

GRADED INSTRUCTION

A child's abilities and needs are different from an adult's, so instruction must be geared according to the unique characteristics of each age. Paul reminded us of this fact when he described his own development. "When I was a child, I talked like a child, I thought like a child, I reasoned like a child. When I became a man, I put childish ways behind me" (1 Cor. 13:11). Jesus, the Master Teacher, was sensitive to the readiness of his disciples. At one point he was not able to teach them what he wanted to (John 16:12). Some lessons had to wait. We too must be sensitive to our learners' readiness.

Below is a list of a few of the characteristics and needs that apply to particular ages. The numbers are approximate and would vary widely from person to person.

Here are a few examples of common mistakes that illustrate the importance of readiness and graded instruction. You are studying some of the stories in the life of Jesus with your second graders. You would like to show them a map of Jesus' travels, but they do not yet know how maps work. All those lines and dots mean nothing to the young child.

65 & up Struggling with continued value and usefulness

40-55 Coping with aging parents

40-50 Coping with teens

35-45 Resetting life goals

25-40 Raising children

20-35 Establishing career

22 Marriage

18-21 Preparation for marriage and family life

16-23 Preparation for life occupation

16 Using more technical and abstract jargon; gaining expertise in specialized areas

14-20 Establishing emotional independence and identity separate from parents and peers

12-17 Concern with sexual adjustment

12-14 Becoming more comfortable with abstract, logical, scientific reasoning; symbolism begins to function more easily

10-20 Establishing a value system and life goals

6-11 (grade school years) Learning more complex linguistic skills (prepositions, passive voice, complex sentences, etc.); learning to read and write; learning to follow more complicated directions; learning to use maps; learning to get along with peers

4-5 Beginning to learn right from wrong

3 Vocabulary approximately 1,000 words with inaccurate understanding of many words (over- and under-extensions)

2-3 Can "obey," but only because of pain and pleasure, not because of any moral reasoning

2 Vocabulary approximately 300 simple words

1 Walk

Suppose that we are studying the trials of Jesus with some third graders. We would like them to understand the interplay between the Jewish authorities and the Roman authorities. But government is still largely a mystery to third graders, and the concept of local rule under foreign occupation is even more difficult.

Suppose we are talking with a three-year-old boy, trying to explain the reasons why he should not steal. But at this age he has difficulty understanding anything other than the immediate punishments or rewards he gets for his actions. A genuine concept of right and wrong usually does not develop until a few years later.

Suppose we would like a preschooler to understand God's goodness. We speak in terms of "historical" examples of God's "providence" and "faithfulness." We describe how God "sustains" his people with so many "provisions" for our "benefit" and "welfare." All of this is very meaningful and inspiring to us, but the preschooler hardly understands a word we say.

We are teaching fourth graders about the church. We describe it as a bride, a building, and a body. But the use of such symbolism is not easily understood by them until several years later.

We are faithfully teaching a junior high or high school class about heroes of the Bible or the outstanding figures of church history, but they are more interested in finding out about dating and sex.

Perhaps we would like our young adults to become more active in leadership positions in the church, so we teach them about the stewardship of talents and the importance of the local church. But they are struggling to raise young children and would like some help with child psychology and family discipline.

We may plan to survey the dispensations or the covenants with our middle adult class, but they need some insights on communicating with their independent-minded teenagers.

We set up a program in which teens will be responsible for doing a variety of things for the senior citizens in the church. But older folks need to have responsibilities. They need to feel needed and useful.

In each of these cases a lesson was planned that was worthwhile in itself. In some cases the lesson came too early, before the child was able to understand. In other cases the lesson was not the one that was most needed by the learners. These two issues, *readiness* and *needs,* are the keys to graded instruction. All of our teaching must be graded according to the level of readiness and the pressing needs of our learners.

COMMUNICATING WITH THE LISTENER IN MIND

Communication can be defined simply as one person conveying meaning to another person. We tend to equate talking with communicating. But if there is no transfer of meaning, there is no communication.

The eight steps in communication are illustrated in the diagram on the next page. (1) The speaker, or sender experiences something (senses something in the environment). (2) He thinks about his experience. This thought, or idea, is what he would like to communicate to another person. (3) Since he has not yet learned how to do direct mind transfer, he must encode his idea in symbolic form (spoken words, written words, gestures, or postures). Encoding is the process of selecting these words, gestures, postures, etc. Encoding usually goes on without much conscious attention, since the message is still internal. (4) Then he expresses the symbols. (5) The symbols are transmitted (with sound and light if he and the receiver are in primary contact, but with additional mechanical or electronic means if they are not in primary contact). (6) The receiver senses the symbols. (7) He decodes them. (8) Finally, he thinks about the meaning of the symbols. *If* the meaning that the receiver gets from the symbols is the same idea that the sender wanted him to think about, then the communication has been a success.

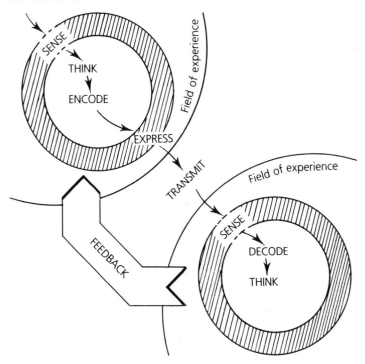

The problem is that there can be a breakdown at any one of the steps between the sender's thought and the receiver's thought. The sender may encode his thought poorly. He may misspeak himself. The transmission, especially if mechanical or electronic means are involved, could become garbled. The receiver may sense only part of what is transmitted. He may then decode the symbols improperly. Even if only one of these problems arises, the communication will not be as effective as it could be. But if several of these problems occur, the receiver is sure to end up with an idea that is quite different from the sender's original idea.

We will examine encoding and decoding, since

these are the areas where serious breakdowns in communication often occur. A person normally encodes and decodes thoughts according to his own field of experience. His field of experience (see diagram) includes everything in his background that has any effect on how he thinks, such as his childhood rearing, his circle of friends, his education, his values, or his vocation. When two people have the same field of experience, their encoding and decoding have the same basis and their communication can be quite efficient. But finding two people with the same field of experience is as unlikely as finding Siamese twins. Usually the sender and receiver have quite different fields of experiences. Thus, the sender must be careful to encode his thoughts with the receiver's field of experience in mind. Or, the receiver must decode the sender's expressions with the sender's field of experience in mind.

The teacher's only safe assumption is that his learners will decode according to the learners' own field of experience. This is obviously true when the learners are children, and almost always true when they are adults. Thus, it is the teacher's responsibility to encode his thoughts according to the learner's field of experience so that when the learner decodes them, he will get the intended idea. The teacher must develop the ability to pretend that he has the same field of experience as his learner and then gear his statements so that they will make immediate sense to the learner.

FEEDBACK AND LISTENING

Feedback, as indicated in the diagram, is the response of the receiver to the message he has just decoded. He becomes the sender and the original sender becomes the receiver. The same sequence of encoding, expressing, transmitting, sensing, and decoding takes place

whichever direction the flow of communication is
moving.

Feedback is vital to effective communication, but
some types of feedback are more helpful than others.
For example, suppose that A says something to B and
then asks, "Did you understand that?" Whether or not B
understood, he will want to say that he did for various
psychological reasons. Even if B ended up with a totally
different idea than A started with, as long as B received
some idea he will probably assume that it was the idea
A sent. Asking someone if he understood a message
sent will uncover a communication breakdown only if
the other person decoded something that was
meaningless to him and only if he is willing to admit it.
When someone is asked if he understood a message,
and he says "Yes," the sender needs to find some other
way to discover whether he really understood or not.

Suppose again that A says something to B. But this
time he asks him to tell him what he just said. So B
repeats the same thing that A said, in the same words.
This may sound like good communication to A, but it
doesn't guarantee a thing. Perhaps B has a good
memory and was able to repeat A's words, but didn't
understand them at all. Or, perhaps B understood
something different than A meant, but by using the
same words A used, he conceals that misunderstanding
from A.

Obviously, the safest way to get feedback is to
encourage the other person to respond in *his own words.*
If the *idea* that comes back is the same *idea* as sent,
even though the words are different, the communication
has probably been successful. *Thus, we should always
encourage our learners to give us plenty of feedback in
their own words.* (Of course, there is also the possibility
that B understands A accurately, but by putting his
response in his own words gives A the impression that
he does not understand. But such a problem is usually

quickly discovered in further exchanges.)

It is easy to see that a very important part of teaching is listening to our learners. And when we are decoding what our learners say, we must do the same thing we do when we are encoding—we must keep the learner's field of experience in mind. Only by empathizing with the learner will we get an accurate idea of what he has in mind.

Unfortunately, we often think that talking is active, while listening is passive. We feel that the speaker is expending effort, but the listener will not expend any effort until it is his turn to talk. But good listening is active listening. It takes a great deal of mental effort to identify with the other person and to interpret his expressions on the basis of his field of experience. It requires effort to listen for the underlying feelings as well as the explicit statements. It requires effort to listen "between the lines." But it is not wasted effort. Careful listening brings significant rewards. It increases our understanding of others. Also, as we adjust our encoding according to what we learn while we are listening, it increases others' understanding of us.

In both of the aspects we have discussed in this section, graded instruction and communication, the key is to *think in terms of the learner.*

PLANNING A LESSON

 PRINCIPLE 24: A teacher should plan each lesson so that the learner is guided through four steps: seeing his own *need*, understanding the biblical *information* that answers that need, *personalizing* that information, and taking *action*.

Whenever a person learns a Bible lesson, whether it comes through a sermon, a Sunday school lesson, a youth meeting, a counseling session, or his own personal study, he will follow the same basic steps. The four steps that are given in the following diagram can be summarized with the four words, *Need, Information, Personalization,* and *Action*. These are the steps the learner goes through, not the teacher.

These four steps are not original with this writer. No doubt, the basic sequence of steps has been understood as long as teachers have thought seriously about teaching. John Dewey described the sequence thoroughly in his discussions of the steps in problem solving. Alan Monroe described five steps in his "motivated sequence" (attention, need, satisfaction, visualization, action). Lois LeBar has three steps (boy, book, boy). Larry Richards came up with hook, book, look, took. And many curriculum publishers have their own catchy way of labeling the same basic sequence.

TEACHER

	Guide him to think about his present life pattern.	Guide him to think about the Bible.	Guide him to think about his changed life pattern.	
PRESENT LIFE PATTERN	① He becomes aware of his *need*. "I have a need in my present life pattern."	② He understands the *Bible information*. "This information answers my need."	③ *He personalizes* the Bible information. "I plan to put this information to work in my life."	④ He *acts* according to his plan and changes his life pattern. — NEW LIFE PATTERN

LEARNER

The teacher and learner are in contact for only a brief time. Then each one goes his own way until the next meeting. During that brief contact the teacher must guide the learner through three important steps so that the learner will continue with the fourth step on his own.

The rationale for these steps is actually quite simple. The second step, the *Information Step,* is obviously necessary because of the fact that cognition always precedes any decision or action that the learner will make. The information is described on the diagram as *Bible information,* because true Christian ministry involves the Bible's teachings. The first step, the *Need Step,* is necessary in order to help the learner see how the Bible information relates to his present life and to motivate him to learn and apply the lesson. This first step is perhaps the most crucial and also the most neglected step. The third step, the *Personalization Step*, is necessary in order to help the learner see what improvements the Bible information can make in his life. And the fourth step, the *Action Step*, takes place when the learner actually puts the lesson to work in his life. All four of these steps are necessary when the aim of the lesson is an action aim. When the aim is a knowledge aim, the lesson is completed with just the first two steps.

Notice on the diagram that the teacher functions as a guide who leads the learner through each step. The teacher might be a pastor giving a sermon, a junior high Sunday school teacher, or a counselor. Nevertheless, he should think of himself as a guide.

THE NEED STEP

The *Need Step* is absolutely essential. If the teacher can guide the learner to see his need, the rest of the lesson will progress with surprising ease. If the teacher doesn't, the rest of the lesson will be wasted. Some teachers consider only the logical order of their lesson. They want to make sure that they cover the material in precisely the correct order. They place prerequisite ideas, definitions, and discussions of background material first. Then they design each following portion of the material to flow logically from what has gone before. But if logical order is the only concern, the lesson is likely to fail. Such logical ordering of the material can be of great advantage during the *Information Step*, but more is needed than that. The other steps are also needed if the psychological order (or motivational order) is taken into account. Perfect logical order will be an asset only if the learner is psychologically prepared for the information. Motivation is more than half the battle.

As we will recall from Principle 6, an individual is already motivated by his organismic needs, but he is not necessarily motivated by his normative needs. As his teacher we have identified a normative need, an area in his life where spiritual growth is needed. We may be aware of this normative need, but he is not. *In order for him to be motivated by that need, he must become aware of the need.* This is one of the basic ways that the organismic needs and normative needs differ. Organismic needs are built in and are automatically motivating because of our biological and psychological makeup. But normative needs do not motivate an individual until he becomes aware of them. Thus, our first, and perhaps most significant, task as his teacher is to gently to make him aware of his need. Once he becomes aware of his need, the Holy Spirit will work directly in his emotions to help him have the proper feelings and desires in connection with that need. When that occurs, he is motivated. The Holy Spirit will faithfully work in his emotions to motivate him, but the teacher must first work on his intellect so he will become aware of his need.

How do we make a person aware of his need? Do we simply tell him, "You need to stop gossiping," or "You ought to witness more," or "You are not as kind as you should be?" What would our reaction be if someone gave us such a direct analysis of our weaknesses and sins? Most people would become defensive. They would either deny their need or point out worse needs in others. Such a direct approach would probably do just the opposite of what we had hoped. So we should be much more gentle and subtle in helping another person see his need.

In order for a person to see his need, he must realize that there is a gap between where he is and where he should be. For example, suppose that one of the learners has a need to study his Bible more. He must see that there is a gap between his present level of Bible study and the level at which he should be.

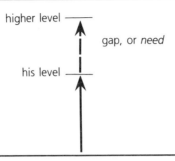

In order to see a gap, a person must see two things: his own lower level of performance and the higher, preferred level of performance. If he has no vision of a higher level, he will not see the need. And, if he does see the higher level, but does not realize that he fails to match up to that higher level, he will also fail to see the need. This suggests two possible ways of helping him see his need.

The first way to help the learner see his need assumes that he accurately knows how well he is doing in a certain area, but doesn't have a vision of anything better. Thus we need to show him what *could be*. In this case, we must give him a vision of a higher level of performance. This can often be done through a study of the example of Christ, or the positive examples of the apostles or prophets. It can also be done through our own example or the testimony and example of others. As he compares himself with these examples, he will get a glimpse of the higher possibilities. No one will have to say to him, "You are not doing as well as so-and-so."

The second way assumes that he realizes there is a higher level of performance, but thinks he is already there. He is not aware that his own level does not match up to the level he envisions. Thus we need to show him the actual lower level where he is. Many times a mild failure experience will help him see his performance as it really is. Or, we can pose a question that he realizes he should be able to answer but cannot. Or we may even use the technique that Nathan used with David (2 Sam. 12:1-7), to help him see an inconsistency between what he believes or claims and what he has done.

Motivating another person is never easy. So when we find a person who already sees his own need, and is thus motivated, we should use the motivation that is already there.

It may be that many more people than we are aware of already realize their needs, but they are simply not willing to open up and let us know about their needs. If we falsely present ourselves as perfect Christians who are always helping out the other guy, we will discourage any honest discussion of weaknesses and sins. But if we admit our own humanness and failings, others will feel much freer to admit the needs they already see and will be more willing to learn about needs of which they are not already aware.

THE INFORMATION STEP

During this step the learner, who by now is aware of his need, deals directly with the biblical information and principles that provide the answer to his need. We should not assume that this is the time to lecture. All sorts of means and methods are possibilities here (including an occasional brief lecture), just as there are hundreds of possibilities during the other steps as well.

If the aim is a knowledge aim, this *Information Step* concludes the lesson.

THE PERSONALIZATION STEP

After the learner focuses his attention on various concepts, ideas, and principles during the *Information Step*, his task during the *Personalization Step* is to make connections between these new insights and his own life and actions. Sometimes this "application" can be done through a series of examples, with which the learner can identify. As each of the examples is discussed, it is wise to point out what they have in common and how they relate to the basic principle learned in the *Information Step*. This will help the learner think of further applications he can make in his own situation, or recognize unexpected events that happen to him as opportunities to apply the principle.

Another way to help the learner make these connections with his daily life is to guide him through a process in which he selects some temptation or event (that he knows is likely to happen to him) which relates to the idea or principle that has been discussed during the *Information Step*. He is then guided to plan out the details of his own application. In this case, the learner, rather than the teacher, is actually deciding upon his own application under the teacher's guidance.

THE ACTION STEP

The *real* application is in daily life. Even though this step takes place after the learner and the teacher part, it is often possible to end the lesson with some prayer or commitment that expresses the intent of the learner.

With some lessons it is also possible for the teacher to do something after the lesson is completed to encourage carry-over. Sometimes the teacher and the learners can apply the lesson together (for instance, if the lesson was about visitation of the sick or shut-in). Sometimes the teacher can send notes or make phone calls to encourage application, or discuss the class members' applications in a subsequent lesson.

LESSON PLANNING FORM

On the following page is a form that can be used to plan a lesson so that it will include the four steps discussed in this chapter. These four steps are the same whether we are planning a sermon to 4,000 people or a camp discussion with five kids.

The right side of the form should be filled out first, as illustrated. The learner is the one who must go through the four steps in order to learn the lesson, so we should spell out the learner's sequence of thoughts first. Then we can fill in the left side of the form with the various methods and techniques we will use and the experiences we want the learner to have. These methods and experiences must be carefully chosen so that they will stimulate the thoughts we have written down in the right column. There are probably dozens of ways to get the learner to think the first thought, dozens of ways for the second and all the other thoughts. Here is where our creativity can flourish. But we must remember that the effectiveness of our methods is judged by how well they bring about the desired thoughts, not by how different or flashy they are.

As we plan a lesson, we will be tempted to focus most of our attention on what we are going to do as the teacher. But this is a mistake. Most of our attention, both in the preparation of the lesson and during the lesson, should be focused on what the learner is thinking.

Lesson Planning Form

Title   FAVORITISM

Topic or Scripture   James 2:1-10

Aim: to show continuing acceptance to someone previously neglected

Name _____

Date _____

Age group   Junior High

Length of session: _____min.

Materials _____

Planner's activities (techniques, questions, etc.) and *learner's experiences*

Individual learner's thoughts (use first person singular)

STEPS

	Individual learner's thoughts	STEPS	
	The people I want most to think well of me are _____, _____, and _____. In order to get them to think well of me, I sometimes give them special treatment. Early Christians did the same thing and they were called "judges with evil motives"! Why is this considered so bad?	N E E D	(Attention) Learner *awareness* of his own need
	Because: 1. It is the opposite of God's example (God does not play favorites). vv. 5-7 2. It is the opposite of love. vv. 8, 9 3. It is inconsistent with my faith and makes me guilty. vv. 1-4, 9, 10 (Sum, or Principle: Favoritism is sin.)	I N F O	Bible study
	By playing favorites I have neglected So-n-so. I could make up for it by . . . (for example: befriending him in the presence of others, or giving him a special invitation to . . .)	P E R S	Use several illustrations or guide learner to select & plan his own application
	Lord, I will invite So-n-so to . . . (actual invitation)	A C T	Decision or commitment Carry-over

METHODS FOR MEANINGFUL INVOLVEMENT

 PRINCIPLE 25: Teaching methods are ways of securing the learner's meaningful involvement in the learning experience and guiding the learner according to the lesson aim.

WHAT IS A METHOD?

Whenever we guide a learner through learning experiences, we guide him in certain ways, which we call teaching methods. Methods, such as discussion, storytelling, and lecture, are simply means to an end. The end, of course, is stated in the aim we have written for the lesson. Guidance is always toward a certain goal, thus methods must always be used with that goal or aim in mind. If we use certain methods just because we like them, or because the equipment is available, we are letting the method become an end in itself. Our method may appear to work smoothly, but if it does not lead to the goal, it is a wasted method. So whenever we use methods, we should choose them and use them with our aim in mind.

No method is good in itself. Saying that a certain method is a good one is like saying that a certain road is a good road. If a road does not take us where we want to go, it is not a good road to use. Likewise, if a method does not take the learners where we want to guide them, it is not a good method to use at that time or for that particular lesson. Visuals can be very helpful in many lessons, but even they become ends in themselves for many teachers. Flannel board, film, and many other visuals are often used for their own sake, even in cases where another method would have been more effective for that particular lesson.

We should always ask ourselves the following questions:

"What result will this method produce?" and "Is there another method that will lead to the aim more effectively?"

USING METHODS WISELY

Methods should focus on the activity of the learner rather than the activity of the teacher. That is, methods are not primarily for the teacher; they are for the learner. The key question is not what the teacher is doing while a certain method is being used, but what the learner is doing.

We want more than mere activity on the part of the learner. We want to secure his *meaningful involvement* in the learning experience. Involvement becomes meaningful when it is direct rather than indirect, when it involves as many of the learner's senses as possible, when it is relevant to the topic and the aim, and when it is appropriate to the learner's readiness and needs. Generally, the higher we go on the chart below, the more meaningful the learner involvement will be.

Any lesson that we plan to teach could be taught in many different ways using many different methods. We

the *whole person* is involved	The learner experiences real life	Service projects, Discovering something in real life, Field trips, Making something, etc.
the *whole person* is involved	The learner imagines he is in a real life situation	Role play, Drama, Demonstration, etc.
hearing words and *seeing* pictures or objects	Someone else tells about and shows representations of real life	Pictures, Films, Models, Objects, etc.
merely *hearing* words	Someone else merely tells about real life	Lecture, Reading a book, etc.

(left margin top: more direct)
(left margin bottom: indirect and vicarious)

should try to find the methods that will involve the learners in the learning experience in the most meaningful way. For example, suppose we want a junior high class to learn how to use a Bible concordance. If we merely use words to describe a concordance and how it can be put to use in Bible study, the class' involvement will not be very meaningful. However, if we bring a concordance and *show* the class how to use it, the students' involvement will be more meaningful because they are seeing as well as hearing. But their experience is still relatively indirect and vicarious. Their involvement would be even more meaningful if we let *them* use it during class time. We could give them a certain word and then let them find all the Bible passages containing that word. But it would be more meaningful still if we let them choose a subject that is already of concern to them. In this way they would be directly using the concordance in a real-life learning experience. And in the future they will then be likely to use a concordance to find out what the Bible says about some of their other concerns—much more than if they had merely heard us describe the use of the concordance. They have learned what we wanted them to learn because we used a method that guaranteed their meaningful involvement.

Whatever method we use, it should not draw attention to itself. For example, object lessons are often so interesting in themselves that they draw attention away from the lesson we are trying to teach. Suppose we are teaching about David's courage and trust in the Lord, and we use a sling as an object lesson. The sling becomes so interesting that the child cannot keep his mind on the real lesson. When he gets home he asks his father to make a sling like David's and forgets everything else from the lesson.

Also, whenever we can, we should use methods that make the learning experience fun. Too much fun, of course, would be distracting; but the overall experience should be enjoyable.

THE MOST MISUSED METHOD

The lecture method may seem like an easy method to use, since we can simply plan what we want to say and then say it. However, lecture by itself seldom secures as much meaningful involvement as our learners need. Often we can increase the level of involvement by using a little lecture with other methods such as visuals and discussion. Often we can get the best level of learner involvement if we avoid lecture entirely and use other methods.

INCREASING YOUR REPERTOIRE OF METHODS

Most teachers are comfortable with only a very few methods. We would be wise to increase our repertoire of methods one at a time. The chart on the next page provides a variety of methods and audiovisual media for various ages. Thirteen of the most basic methods are indicated with an asterisk (*). We should try to master these more basic methods first.

A SUMMARY OF IMPORTANT STEPS
IN PREPARING A LESSON

1. *Identify the need.*
    a. If we are using *prepared* materials: Study the main thrust of the lesson. Then review the learners' spiritual needs (from the teacher's notebook) to see if most of the learners have a similar need that could be met by the given lesson. Write down that need.
    b. If *not* using prepared materials, or if most of the learners have a spiritual need which is more urgent than the need dealt with in the prepared materials: Write down the urgent need. Then select a Bible passage related to that need and briefly study the main thrust of that passage.
2. *Write the aim,* being careful to determine whether a knowledge aim or an action aim is most appropriate. Then, if it is an action aim, write down each learner's name and how he should apply the lesson. Be specific.
3. *Study the Bible.* Make an in-depth study of the Bible passage (and/or other material). Make notes as you study.
4. *Plan the lesson.*
    a. Ponder the learners' current motivations, feelings about the lesson, and interests. What do they already know about the lesson?
    b. Fill in all parts of your lesson plan. (See the lesson planning form under the discussion of Principle 24.)   (cont.)

61 Teaching Methods and Media for Various Age Groups

Method	2-3	4-5	6-8	9-11	12 & up
1. *Assignment—academic (read & report)				x	x
2. *Assignment—active (do/observe & report)	x	x	x	x	x
3. Audio aids (records-tapes)	x	x	x	x	x
4. Brainstorming				x	x
5. Buzz groups (& 2x2 discussing)				x	x
6. Case studies, case histories			x	x	x
7. *Chalkboard			x	x	x
8. Charts, diagrams				x	x
9. Conversation	x	x	x	x	x
10. Choral reading			x	x	x
11. Current events				x	x
12. Debates					x
13. Demonstration	x	x	x	x	x
14. *Direct Bible study				x	x
15. Drawing, charting	x	x	x	x	x
16. Duplicated handouts			x	x	x
17. Field trips		x	x	x	x
18. Films			x	x	x
19. Filmstrips, slides		x	x	x	x
20. Flash cards	x	x	x	x	
21. *Flannelgraph	x	x	x	x	(x)
22. Flipchart			x	x	x
23. Games	x	x	x	x	x
24. *Group discussion			x	x	x
25. Handwork	x	x	x	x	
26. Identification with persons, events (feelings)		x	x	x	x
27. *Illustration (practical examples)		x	x	x	x
28. Interest centers	x	x	x	x	
29. Interview				x	x
30. *Lecture					x
31. Listening teams			x	x	x
32. Making things (murals, displays, etc.)	x	x	x	x	x
33. Maps, globe				x	x
34. Memorization	x	x	x	x	x
35. Models & objects	x	x	x	x	x
36. Music, Art, Poetry, Literature (all the arts)	x	x	x	x	x
37. Open-ended methods		x	x	x	x
38. Object lessons (beware!)				x	x
39. *Overhead projector			x	x	x
40. Motion songs, finger play, etc.	x	x			
41. Notebook, notetaking					x
42. Panels, Forums, Symposiums					x
43. Picture studies	x	x	x	x	x
44. Playing Bible stories	x	x	x		
45. *Problem solving			x	x	x
46. *Projects (individual, group)			x	x	x
47. Puppets	x	x	x	x	
48. *Question-answer	x	x	x	x	x
49. Resource person				x	x
50. Review	x	x	x	x	x
51. Rhetorical question			x	x	x
52. Role playing & simulation (acting out life situations, unrehearsed)		x	x	x	x
53. Paraphrasing Scripture			x	x	x
54. Silent thinking			x	x	x
55. Skits, Drama, Tableau, Pantomime				x	x
56. *Storytelling	x	x	x	x	x
57. Team Teaching		x	x	x	x
58. Television (videotape)		x	x	x	x
59. Test, quiz			x	x	x
60. Testimony				x	x
61. Workbook			x	x	x

Adapted from Lawrence Richards, *The Key to Sunday School Achievement* (Moody, 1965), p. 36.

    c. Remember to integrate every part of the lesson around the aim.

    d. In choosing methods, remember to think in terms of the learners' meaningful involvement and variety.

    e. Allow for plenty of feedback throughout the lesson.

    f. Think through the lesson as a learner. Are you accomplishing your aim?

5. *Prepare Materials* (visuals, handouts, etc.).

6. *Practice.* Imagine your learners before you. Ask yourself: What are they thinking? How do they respond? Check your timing so you don't include too much.

7. After you give the lesson, *Evaluate.* Did you accomplish the aim? Why or why not? How can you improve the next lesson?

EIGHT
THE LOCAL CHURCH, THE LIVING ORGANISM OF CHRISTIAN MINISTRY

THE NATURE AND MISSION OF THE LOCAL CHURCH

 PRINCIPLE **26:** **The church is a body of saved people, people scattered to evangelize the lost, people gathered to edify one another, and people regrouped into various agencies to carry out specialized ministries.**

THE WORD "CHURCH"

Throughout the New Testament the word "church" (Greek: *ekklesia*) is used to refer to people. We would do well to remember that, but we easily forget. One of the reasons we forget that the church is people is that our English word "church" is typically used today to refer to organizations and programs of either one local church or the denomination as a whole. And when we say that we are going to stop and visit the pastor at the church, we are referring to the church as the building. Of course, such usages are common and completely legitimate today. However, in the New Testament the word "church" *(ekklesia)* was never used to refer to a building, organization, or program. In the New Testament "church" always refers to people.

The Greek word *ekklesia* (which literally means

"called out ones") is nearly identical to our word "group" in its meaning and usage. The context of each use of this word in the New Testament usually distinguishes this group from other groups by indicating their positive relationship to Jesus or to God. Thus, perhaps the simplest and shortest definition of the local church is that it is a *group of saved people.*

THE NATURE OF THE CHURCH

To expand our short definition of the local church we could say that it is *a group of professing Christians in a given locality regularly involved in Christian interaction.* Ideally, the local church is merely a space-time segment of the universal church. In other words, since the universal church is composed of all true Christians in all places throughout the entire age of the church, each local church should be a subgroup of the universal church interacting in just one place during one period of time. Realistically, however, a local church may not involve every Christian in its locality, and it may involve some who are not really Christians. Nevertheless, we will consider the local church to be composed primarily of true Christians. The significance of the "Christian interaction" mentioned in the definition will be explained in the next section.

Is the church (the "called out ones") only a church when the people are called out to a meeting? No. The fact that *ekklesia* stands for "called out ones" signifies only that they are called out of the world and called into the family of God, or into Christ. In fact, the New Testament refers to various groups of saved people as "church" even when the people are scattered (Acts 8:3; 14:27; 1 Cor. 14:23).

THE MISSION OF THE CHURCH

What is the mission, or purpose, of the church? Since

the church remains the church both while its people are gathered and while they are scattered, our question about the mission of the church can be asked in two ways. First, what is the purpose of the church when it is scattered? And second, what is the purpose of the church when it is gathered? In other words, what should Christians be doing when they are spread out in the community as individuals? And why should Christians meet with each other?

Since all ministry is aimed at fulfilling needs, these two questions can be answered very easily by noting the needs of the people involved. Nonbelievers need to become Christians. So when the church is scattered among nonbelievers, its mission is to evangelize them. In contrast, Christians do not need to be evangelized, but they do need to grow toward Christlikeness. So when the church is gathered and Christians are interacting with other Christians, its mission is to edify each of the believers and encourage their spiritual growth. In short, the church's reason for existence is twofold: evangelism when the church is scattered, edification when the church is gathered. Evangelism has been discussed under our study of Principles 8—16. The key elements which make up edification are discussed in the next section.

EVANGELISM, EDIFICATION, AND SOCIAL WORK

Which is more important, evangelism, edification, or social work? Each one is required by the New Testament.

Support for evangelism	Support for edification	Support for social work
Jesus' example, Matt. 28:19; Eph. 4:11; Acts 13:2, 3.	Jesus' example; Matt. 28:20; Eph. 4:11; Acts 15:36.	Jesus' example; James 1:27; 1 Tim. 5:3-16; Luke 9:2; Gal. 6:10.

As pictured in the diagram below, evangelism involves a Christian (someone who is already part of the church) reaching out to a non-Christian for the express purpose of explaining the gospel and inviting him to become a Christian (come into the church). Edification involves a Christian ministering to another Christian (who is already part of the church). And social work involves a Christian reaching out to help a non-Christian cope with life and live with dignity even though he remains outside the church. (Of course, social work can also take place within the church, as mentioned in Galatians 6:10.)

Each of these three elements affects, and is affected by, the other two. A person cannot be edified before he is evangelized. Yet a person who has been edified (and thus has grown spiritually) will be more effective in evangelism. Also, engaging in evangelism edifies a person (helps him grow spiritually). Social work, although it is not done for ulterior reasons, still opens many opportunities for both evangelism and edification.

Thus, in various ways these three activities are interdependent.

The local church cannot pick out one of these three activities and say that it will limit its ministry to that one. The church must engage in all three. Of course, the church will also have to decide which one or ones must be emphasized, depending on the needs in the church and in the community. But the church must never neglect any one of these three activities. Balance is the rule.

However, as far as the individual Christian is concerned, balance is not as important. Individuals are gifted in some areas much more than in other areas, so some individuals, for instance, may do much edification and little social work, or much evangelism and little edification. The individual should devote most of his ministry to the specific areas where he feels he is most effective. Gearing his ministry according to his own gifts and abilities is more important than trying to achieve a perfect balance. However, when dozens or hundreds of individual Christians are found together in one local church, the three activities of the whole church will be much more balanced.

THE CHURCH AND THE FAMILY

The Bible teaches that God has established three agencies: the family, civil government, and the church. Besides these three, Christians have established numerous other agencies. What is the place of the church among all these agencies? First we will look at the church and the family.

In Old Testament times God's two nurturing agencies were the family and the system of worship and culture God gave to the nation of Israel. In New Testament times God's two nurturing agencies are the family and the local church. These two agencies are quite similar in their purpose and their potential. They should be viewed as complementary rather than competitive. Nevertheless, each one has something unique to offer. The home is especially suited to the evangelism and nurture of children, and bears most of the responsibility for that. The church is especially suited to the evangelism and nurture of adults, and bears most of the responsibility for that. The gradual shift in responsibility throughout the life of an individual is pictured in the diagram below.

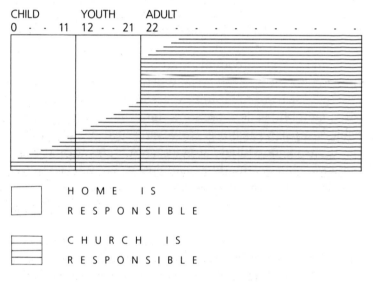

CHILD   YOUTH   ADULT
0 - - 11 12 - - 21 22 - - - - - - - - - - -

☐   H O M E   I S   R E S P O N S I B L E

☰   C H U R C H   I S   R E S P O N S I B L E

The home and the church are mutually inter-dependent. The church can help the home greatly by electing officers and leaders who are pleasing God in their family lives and who are sensitive to the needs of families. The church can also allow the family to have more time together. And through its various programs the church can give adults the practical help they need to be effective partners and parents. The healthier the families, the healthier the church. And vice versa.

THE CHURCH AND "OTHER" AGENCIES

The church includes many agencies, some within the traditional program of the local church and some outside.

Agencies Often Found as Subgroupings of the Local Church	"Para-church" Agencies
Sunday school Children's church Children's clubs Youth groups Women's groups etc.	Children's clubs (e.g., CEF) Youth organizations (e.g., Youth For Christ, Inter-Varsity, Campus Crusade) Mission boards (e.g., The Evangelical Alliance Mission, Sudan Interior Mission) Camps and Conferences Schools (elementary, secondary, colleges, seminaries) Radio and Television broadcasters Publishers Traveling seminars etc.

The various agencies listed in the right column are commonly called parachurch agencies, but that label is most unfortunate. Instead, they should be referred to as "arms" or "branches" of the church. "Para" means beyond or alongside. If these agencies are truly alongside the church, then they are not part of the church. But these agencies really are part of the church just as a branch is part of a tree. They may not be part of any one local church, but they are certainly part of the universal church. They are believers who are regrouped and organized in highly specialized ways to carry out part of the church's great commission. Just as local churches are geographical groupings of the universal church, these agencies are also groupings of the universal church. Their makeup and purpose may be outside the traditional *program* of the local church. Their specific mission is more specialized and they usually draw their personnel from various local churches. But these facts should not make us think of them as outside the church.

Just as the family and the local church are interdependent, so are the local church and these many branch agencies. The trunk needs its branches and the branches need their trunk. Neither can take the place of the other. They must learn to cooperate and not compete. There is a constant need for communication and mutual support between the various groupings of the church—the family, the local church with its many local agencies, and the many branches of the church.

KEY ELEMENTS IN THE LIFE OF THE CHURCH

 PRINCIPLE 27: Christians should gather for instruction and mutual edification. Regular Christian interaction is the life of the church.

The activities that make up the life of the local church can be divided into two main categories: evangelism and edification. Edification can be further divided into such elements as instruction, worship, fellowship, service, and prayer. Every church should include all of these elements on a regular basis. One more element, *discipline*, should be practiced whenever the need arises. The regular elements are illustrated in the life of the first church in Jerusalem (Acts 2:41-47) and most of them are commanded in other passages (Matt. 28:19, 20; Eph. 4:11-16; Heb 10:24, 25). A balanced church program will include all of these overlapping activities.

In this section we focus our attention on three of these elements: instruction, fellowship, and service. We also carefully consider the purpose of meetings. The element of worship is discussed under Principle 28. The place of music is discussed under Principle 29.

INSTRUCTION: THE MOST BASIC ELEMENT

Instruction, or teaching, forms the logical basis for every other activity that makes up the life of the local church. As illustrated in the diagram below, proper instruction (instruction that is biblical, balanced, and applied) will eventually lead to all the other elements.

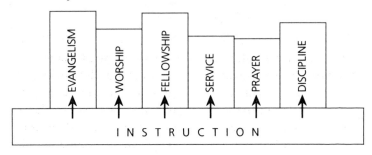

However, the same thing cannot be said for any of the other elements. Each of the other elements is dependent upon instruction. If there is no instruction, how will we know what message to give to the lost and how to go about evangelism? If there is no instruction, how will we know whom we worship and how to worship? If there is no instruction, how will we know what real fellowship is, how to go about service, how to pray and what to pray for, and whom and how to discipline? Instruction logically precedes all the other elements.

When we say that instruction precedes the other elements, we are referring to logical order. In regard to chronological order, evangelism obviously precedes all the elements that make up edification. In regard to psychological order, fellowship probably precedes the other elements. But in regard to the element which is the logical prerequisite to all the others, instruction comes first.

When a church neglects teaching, it destroys the foundation of all the other elements. They will eventually disappear or become improper and unbalanced. This means that each church must give careful regard to its instruction. The church leaders (pastors/elders) must be "able to teach" (1 Tim. 3:2). And the educational program of the church must be one of the church's top priorities.

THE PURPOSE OF MEETINGS

Why should Christians gather? As described under Principle 26, the purpose of the church gathered is edification. But this is only a general answer to the question of the purpose for gathering. Because of the importance of instruction in the life of the local church, we can be more specific and say that Christians should meet with each other in order to be edified through instruction. And, since the pastors or elders of the church are required to be "able to teach," it seems appropriate that they do most of the teaching. But that in itself is still an inadequate answer to the question. While it is true that Christians should gather in order to be taught by the church leaders, the New Testament also emphasizes another reason to meet.

In two different passages Christians are told that they should meet with other Christians, not merely to receive a ministry performed by others, but to minister to others. The writer of Hebrews states that Christians should go to church meetings in order to *give* something. "Let us consider how we may spur one another on toward love and good deeds. Let us not give up meeting together . . . but let us encourage one another" (Heb. 10:24, 25). Note that this command is in the active voice. It does not say that we should meet in order to be spurred on toward love and good deeds, or to be encouraged. Rather, we are the ones who are ministering to others by encouraging and spurring them on. This is not merely a meeting in which the ministry is one-way, from the pastor or teacher to the rest of the people. If each Christian comes to the meeting and carries out this command, all the believers will be building up each other. This is not just edification; this is *mutual edification*. Paul also emphasized mutual edification when he told the Corinthian believers to come to their meetings prepared to speak up. "When you come together, everyone has a hymn, or a word of instruction, a revelation, a tongue or an interpretation. All of these must be done for the strengthening of the church" (1 Cor. 14:26).

Unfortunately, most Christians think of themselves as listeners at church. But the New Testament view is that each believer is an active participant. The church is viewed as an *organism* made up of mutually interdependent parts. The church needs the contribution of each person just as a body depends on the functioning of each different part. Paul made a major point of this in an extended discussion of the church as a body (1 Cor. 12:12-30). He also emphasized the importance of each individual's contribution when he said that "the whole body . . . grows and builds itself up in love, *as each part does its work*" (Eph. 4:16).

Thus, church meetings have a dual purpose: instruction and mutual edification. Every local church should maintain a pattern of activities which includes plenty of instruction and plenty of mutual edification. In other words, there should be regular opportunities for the people to learn from the teaching of their pastors or elders, and there should be regular opportunities for the people to meet in small groups where they can build up one another.

If Christians are going to have anything to share when they meet, they must be studying and applying their Bibles on a regular basis. Mutual edification meetings must not be allowed to degenerate into mutual gossip meetings, or endless theological debates, or merely sharing of opinions. They must center around the Bible. This means that the development of individual Bible study is an important skill for each believer to work at. Mutual edification meetings can be truly beneficial if each person comes to the meeting already having carefully studied a certain scriptural passage or topic.

DO WE MEET IN ORDER TO WORSHIP AND PRAY?

Even though we typically label our regular church meetings "worship services" and "prayer meetings," we are never commanded in the New Testament to meet in order to worship or to pray. While it is true that we will certainly worship and pray when we get together as believers, these are not the reasons for gathering. An analogy may clarify the point. No one goes to a committee meeting in order to breathe. Since breathing is a natural and continuous part of life, however, we will certainly breathe while we are at a committee meeting. Likewise, worship and prayer should be a spontaneous and frequent part of the Christian's life. So Christians will certainly worship and pray both when they are alone and when they are meeting with other Christians. But neither worship nor prayer is the reason for meeting. The fact that we use the words "worship" and "prayer" to label our regular church meetings shows how dependent we are on tradition.

Some insist that we should go to church to meet God. They may even feel that God is present in a church meeting in a special sense, that he is more available or more at work when Christians gather than when they are scattered. This mistaken notion probably arises from four sources.

First, it may be a hangover from the Roman Catholic notion that there is a special presence of Christ in the Eucharist (Holy Communion). But the New Testament clearly teaches that the bread and wine which are used in a communion service are symbols meant to cause believers to remember the Lord's substitutionary death (1 Cor. 11:23-26). Christ is no more present in the Eucharist than he is in any other experience of life or worship.

Second, many Christians mistakenly take Old Testament passages about God's presence in the temple and apply them to our times. While it is true that there was a time when Old Testament saints were commanded to go to the temple for sacrifice and worship because God was present in the temple in a special sense, according to Jesus that old arrangement has been changed (John 4:19-24). God does not indwell a building today. Instead he indwells each individual believer.

Third, some people take Jesus' promise that "where two or three come together in my name, there am I with them" (Matt. 18:20) and assume that Jesus was talking about church meetings. Rather, Jesus was reminding his disciples that he would be with them to give them special help when they had to carry out church discipline, which is always difficult because it requires both boldness and readiness to forgive. (Verse 20 must be interpreted in the light of its context, which includes verses 15-35. Especially compare verse 20 with verse 16.)

Fourth, evangelical and conservative Christians may be reacting to liberal churches, whose meetings can be no more than social gatherings because they deny the personal existence of God. In contrast, we affirm the personal existence of God, and we worship him and talk (pray) to him when we are in our church meetings. But that does not mean that we should overreact and say that we go to church to meet God. As evangelicals and conservatives we believe in both the indwelling of the Holy Spirit and the priesthood of each believer. We have the Lord's presence continually and we can talk with him at any time. We, more than any other group, should realize that we do not have to go to church to meet God in either worship or prayer. Instead, we go to church to interact with other Christians.

We must remember that both worship and prayer are forms of interaction between us and God. In contrast, instruction, fellowship, and service are forms of interaction between us and other Christians. We cannot instruct, fellowship, or serve without interacting with someone else. This is why we meet, to interact with fellow Christians in instruction and mutual edification. Of course, while we are meeting and talking with our fellow believers, we will also talk to the Lord in worship and prayer because such divine interaction comes naturally to Christians whether they are scattered or gathered.

CHRISTIAN FELLOWSHIP

Fellowship is shared experience. The experience can be shared in the sense that several people go through the experience together. Or it can be "shared" in the sense that one person tells another person about his experience.

Christian fellowship is shared *Christian* experience. Human fellowship is shared *human* experience. But these two are often confused. The conversation about the weather over coffee and doughnuts that takes place in "fellowship hall" is not really Christian fellowship at all. It is merely human fellowship. Any person, whether he is a Christian or not, can eat, drink, and talk about the weather. It does not become Christian fellowship until the experience that is shared is a Christian experience. Some people assume that whenever two Christians have fellowship, it is automatically Christian fellowship. But it all depends on the activity or experience that is being shared.

Since Christians are both human and Christian, they need both human fellowship and Christian fellowship. Human fellowship should not be confused with worldliness or friendship with the world. There are many neutral activities that Christians can enjoy with non-Christians. Such human fellowship is fulfilling for both the Christian and the non-Christian, and it builds a basis for mutual trust and sharing of the gospel. Christians also benefit from human fellowship with other Christians.

But nothing can take the place of genuine Christian fellowship between fellow believers. Such Christian fellowship is facilitated in small groups, whereas large groups tend to be impersonal. Small groups have a great potential for intimate fellowship around the Bible and prayer and discussion of the Christian walk. People get to know each other much better in a small group. The interaction is much deeper and more meaningful. In time, mutual respect and trust grow deep. The individual's willingness to open up and expose his true thoughts and feelings always takes time, but it will happen much more easily in a small group than a large one.

Some people say that they like a small church better than a large one. But, of course, the real question is not the overall size of the church. Rather, the question is the level of interaction and fellowship that is present. A small church *can* be cold. A large church *can* have many functioning subgroups in which genuine fellowship and edification occur.

SPIRITUAL GIFTS FOR SERVICE

A wide variety of spiritual gifts are mentioned in Scripture. Some of these gifts could be called "sign gifts"

since they were more obviously miraculous in nature.
They were used primarily to establish the authority of
the apostles. Other spiritual gifts, which we will call
"service gifts" continue to function today as a necessary
part of the life of every church. In this section we will
consider only service gifts.

A service gift may be defined as a Christian's Spirit-
directed and Spirit-powered use of his ability to make a
contribution to the spiritual birth or growth of others.
The main Scripture passages which teach about service
gifts are Romans 12:3-8; 1 Corinthians 12:1-31; and
Ephesians 4:11-16. These passages list a wide variety of
service gifts, including prophesying, serving, teaching,
encouraging, contributing, leadership, showing mercy,
wisdom, knowledge, faith, the ability to distinguish
between spirits, the ability to speak in different
languages, the ability to interpret different languages,
evangelism, and pastoring.

What makes a spiritual gift spiritual? The gifts listed
above are spiritual in two ways. First, spiritual gifts are
God-given abilities. Some gifts, such as faith and the
ability to distinguish between spirits, are probably
given more directly to the individual when he becomes
a Christian. Others, such as serving, teaching,
contributing, and leadership are probably given to
individuals in a more indirect manner. They are the
result of a long series of experiences, perhaps extending
back to childhood, which gradually develop certain
abilities the individual can use to serve others when he
becomes a Christian. The rain which falls upon the
unrighteous is considered one of God's gifts (Matt. 5:45);
so it also seems appropriate to consider the abilities
which an unsaved person develops to be God's gifts.
Thus, all spiritual gifts are God-given; some are
spiritual abilities received more directly from God, while
others are more natural abilities received indirectly from
God.

The second way in which spiritual gifts are spiritual has to do with the *use* of the gift rather than the gift or the ability itself. If the gift is used with the proper motivation and intent, it makes a spiritual contribution. That is why the definition refers to a spiritual gift as something that is used in a Spirit-directed and Spirit-powered way. Even a natural ability which is used under the guidance and power of the Holy Spirit, and thus is used for edifying another person and for glorifying the Lord rather than for selfish reasons, becomes a spiritual gift.

Many Christians make the mistake of asking themselves the question, "What is my spiritual gift?" and then look for some strange mystical power. Instead, we should ask ourselves, "What are my abilities?" and then use them under the Holy Spirit's direction and power to make a contribution to the spiritual birth and growth of others.

This self-examination will require two things. First, we must know ourselves. We must honestly appraise both our abilities and inabilities. We can gradually increase our abilities through study, training, and experience. Second, we must know the needs of the group we want to serve. As we compare the group's needs with our abilities, we will probably find at least one way and perhaps several ways we can serve them. One group may need insight into some Bible passage, and we may be able to share some of our knowledge about that passage. So with that group our spiritual gift is the gift of knowledge. But another group, which includes several people who know more about the Bible than we do, may need something different. And if we have the ability to match their need, then that particular ability is our spiritual gift to them. Thus, which gifts we exercise depends both on what abilities we have and on what the people around us need.

Spiritual gifts are always used for the good of others

and for the glory of God, which requires a humble, yet honest, assessment of our own abilities. It also requires a *continual sensitivity* to the needs of those around us. The more static view of service gifts, which tells us to look for our one or two special abilities and call them our gifts, does not require this continual sensitivity. The view that is being recommended here is a more dynamic view of service gifts because one's gift or gifts in any particular context depends on the needs of the group, and different groups have different needs. Each believer may have several dozen abilities to call upon, but each context of service will call for only one or two of those many abilities. In every situation we should say to ourselves *both*, "What do they need?" and "How may I help?"

INTERACTION

Everything that has been discussed in this section (instruction, mutual edification, fellowship, and gifts) involves interaction. We have defined the local church as a group of professing Christians in a given locality *regularly involved in Christian interaction*. Interaction for the purpose of edifying Christians is what the gathered church is all about.

Having our name on the church roll is not interaction. Attending meetings in which we merely sit and listen is not interaction. Some churches are dead because their doctrine is not biblical. But, unfortunately, some churches which have conservative and evangelical doctrine are also dead because their people are not interacting.

WORSHIP

 PRINCIPLE 28: Worship is expressing God's worth. What we say to God by our words or our actions must spring from what we say to him silently, which in turn must spring from what we know to be true about him.

We use the word "worship" often, but sometimes we are at a loss when we attempt to define it.

Is worship an *awareness?* (If it is, then we could define worship as some scholars do: "Worship is the *acknowledgment* of the divine perfections.")

Is worship an *attitude?* (If so, we could define worship as "an *appreciation* of God's greatness.")

Is worship a *feeling?* (If worship is a feeling, then perhaps worship is best defined in terms of *a sense of God's presence,* or in terms of *feeling close to God.)*

Is worship an *experience?* (Is it the experience that some people speak of as *getting to know God?)*

Is worship *saying something?* (If so, then none of these earlier ideas is correct.)

Is worship *doing something?* (If so, then what must one do?)

In order to answer these questions and to define worship, we will first look at the Hebrew and Greek words in the Bible that are translated "worship." Then we should study what Jesus said about worship, and consider some of the implications for our own personal worship experiences and for the place of worship in the life of the local church.

THE BIBLICAL WORDS FOR WORSHIP

We will recall the sequence of inner functions: impression, personal functions (intellectual, emotional, and volitional), and expression (see Principle 5). If we keep this sequence in mind, we will easily see the significance of the Hebrew and Greek words discussed in this section.

What are the literal meanings of the principal Hebrew and Greek words translated "worship" in our Bibles? The Old Testament word used to speak of the worship of God, *shachah*, means "to bow self down." *Proskuneo*, the principal New Testament word for the worship of God, means "to bow down or to kiss the hand toward." Obviously "bowing down" and "kissing the hand toward" are *expressions*. They are not merely awarenesses or feelings. By comparing the meanings of these two words with the sequence of inner functions, we conclude that worship is the response or the output. To be sure, this output is an expression which arises from input, awareness, feeling, and decision. But *worship does not exist until there is expression.*

Thus, we should define worship in terms of expression. Here is a suggested definition: *Worship is my voluntary, conscious expression to God of his worth, greatness, and goodness to me.*

WHAT JESUS SAID ABOUT WORSHIP

In the Gospel of John, we read that Jesus taught that expressions of worship would no longer be restricted to a certain location. According to the law, under which Jesus lived, worship was tied to a particular city (Jerusalem) and to a particular building (the temple). But the new arrangement would not have those restrictions (John 4:20-24). Later Paul wrote that *we* worship in the Spirit of God and do not rely on the external expressions demanded by the law (Phil. 3:3).

Jesus also taught that our worship must be *in spirit and truth* (John 4:23, 24). But what does it mean to worship in spirit? And what does it mean to worship in truth?

For one thing, it seems safe to assume that worship in spirit does not refer to some thoughtless experience of going through an empty ritual. But even in our so-called informal churches we do have our rituals.

Walk.
Sit.
Choir.
Stand.
Always the same; isn't it bland.
Hymn.
News.
Solo.
Prayer.
Always the same; you've been there.
One.
Two.
Three.
Review.
Always the same; déjà vu.
Stand.
Sing.
Walk.
Talk.
Always the same.

Such monotonous uniformity and thoughtless repetition is a violation of the idea of "conscious expression," as mentioned in the definition of worship. If we are not consciously active in our worship, it is not true worship. Paul alluded to this when he wrote, "I will sing with my spirit, but I will also sing with my mind" (1 Cor. 14:15).

But let's suppose that our minds are awake and active. The expressions that spring from our awareness of God can be expressed in three different ways: mentally, vocally, and behaviorally. The *mental* expression is done in our thoughts, rather than externally, as is silent prayer. The *vocal* expression comes when we speak or sing out loud to God. The *behavioral* expression lets our actions do the talking. We express God's worth, greatness, and goodness by what we do.

If there is a contradiction between our internal expression and our external expression, then we are guilty of deception. If there is a contradiction between what we say and what we do, then we are hypocrites. Any "worship" that is so chopped up that there is a discrepancy between the mental, vocal, and behavioral expressions certainly cannot be properly called worshiping in the spirit.

Furthermore, if there is a contradiction between my expressions and my beliefs, then again I am not worshiping in spirit. If I am to worship in spirit, there must be a positive continuity between what I believe (my awareness or knowledge of God) and what I express. There must also be a positive continuity between what I express silently, vocally, and behaviorally.

There is a practical principle here: I must let my external worship arise from my mental worship, and I must let my mental worship arise from my awareness of God. In other words, what I say to God by my words or my actions must spring from what I say to him silently; and what I say to him silently must spring from what I know to be true about him.

This brings us to the question: What does it mean to worship God in truth? The sequence of human functions reminds us that worship, since it is an expression, is always a response to knowledge. Knowledge about God's worth is a prerequisite to expression of God's worth. People who do not know about God cannot worship him. Also, people who have a *false* knowledge of God cannot worship him in truth. The sequence of human functions also reminds us that input or instruction about God is a prerequisite to both knowledge of God and worship of God.

KNOWLEDGE OF GOD AND WORSHIP ARE NOT MYSTICAL

At this point let us examine the phrases "knowledge of God," and "knowing God personally." Sometimes these phrases are used to describe something that is supposedly quite different from knowledge *about* God—not only far different, but supposedly far better. But knowing God personally should not be separated from knowing about God. Indeed, we must know *about* God, and then *respond* to what we know. As we read the Bible, we learn about God's character, about his actions, about his desires and plans, about what he loves and hates. Furthermore, what we learn about God is very personal *to us*, for what he plans, and what he desires, and what he expects has to do with us. When we respond to what God says, we are responding personally to him.

Thus, two elements must always be linked together in our thinking. The first is knowledge about God, and the second is personal response to that knowledge. The first is a prerequisite to the second; the second is expected to follow from the first. When we respond positively to what we know *about* God, we truly are growing in our personal knowledge of God.

A problem arises, however, since many people think that knowledge of God comes from an innate, direct experience with God that *bypasses* knowledge *about* God. Such direct "contact" *apart from biblical revelation about God* is the essence of mysticism. This mystical "contact" sounds very spiritual, but it is heretical. When we have genuine, personal contact with God because we read what the Bible says and respond to it, we are having a spiritual experience, but not a mystical experience. It is a spiritual experience because we are spirits (or, we have a spirit) and we are interacting with God who also is spirit.

We should not seek mystical experiences. We should not seek God *beyond* the Bible. Rather, we should seek to know God personally by responding to the personal things he has told us to do. Such knowledge of God (the legitimate kind) will always stem from knowledge about God as contained in the Bible. Any so-called contact with God that is not based on what the Bible says is in reality no contact at all, at least no contact with God! The person who seeks God without the aid of the Bible should be warned that he is opening himself to the trickery and deception of the devil. Remember Eve. She sought knowledge of divine things (good and evil), and when she set aside the command of God she unknowingly had only Satan to deal with. Even if we think we see an angel of light, beware, "for Satan himself masquerades as an angel of light" (2 Cor. 11:14).

A parallel idea exists in connection with worship. There is nothing mystical about true worship. Worship is spiritual, but not mystical. In its simplest form, worship means telling or showing God how important we think he is. And there is nothing mystical about that! Worship is similar to knowing God personally in the sense that both are dependent on knowledge about God. A person must know something about God's worth, greatness, and goodness before he can worship God. He gains this knowledge about God through biblical instruction or input.

IMPLICATIONS FOR PERSONAL
AND CHURCH WORSHIP

The fact that input must precede output should be applied practically to our worship services. Those elements which supply input (such as the pastor's sermon) should precede those outward expressions of our worship (such as prayer or congregational singing).

Let us think for a moment about the selection of songs for worship. Not every song that talks about worship is really a worship song. When we sing "Praise the Savior, ye who know him," we are not worshiping so much as we are *exhorting* others to worship. On the other hand, when we sing "Jesus, the very thought of thee," we *are* worshiping. The first song is addressed to others about God; the second song addresses God directly. Remember that we defined worship as an "expression *to God.*" In that light, it is easy to see why only the second song is truly a worship song.

Expressions of worship should not be limited to church buildings. Anywhere you can think, speak, or act, you can also worship. And that worship can be in spirit and truth.

Furthermore, there are many *types* of genuine worship. When a person claps his hands above his head as he sings, is that really worship? If that is *his way* of consciously expressing God's worth, then it is real worship. If an act of kindness is done as a conscious expression of God's worth, it is genuine worship. If I restrain myself from copying a neighbor's quiz answer, and if this is consciously done as an expression of God's worth to me, it is worship. If I work hard at my sport and that hard work is consciously an expression of God's worth to me, that is worship. If I sing a song that praises the character of God and if I mean what I sing, that is worship. If I say silently to God, "You are my guide, I need you," that is worship. If I teach a Sunday school class *because* of God's worth to me, that is worship.

Worship takes many forms. When some other Christian worships, his communication is primarily from him *to God*, not to us. He and God will be able to tell whether or not his worship is in spirit and truth, but we will not. Certainly we will not be justified in condemning his worship just because his form of expression is foreign to us. Jesus warned against such foolishness when he said, "Do not judge according to appearance" (John 7:24).

One more question seems appropriate. Is there such a thing as a worship atmosphere? In one sense there is, and in another sense there isn't. It is true that the atmosphere, or environment, affects people, and this effect can be seen in a number of ways.

First, there is the effect of *association*. Because of certain surroundings (such as a church auditorium, or a flat rock near a quiet lake), some people might be caused to think about God because of previous experiences at those locations. Thus, because we remember, and because we form associations, our surroundings can provide some input for worship.

Second, there is the effect of *sequencing*. Because the congregation always rises to sing the doxology at the beginning of the service, we might also rise and sing. But such singing, caused by the sequence of events in our environment, is not necessarily any higher an activity than an unconscious conditioned reflex. And, if it is unconscious, it is not worship.

The combination of these two aspects of the environment (association and sequencing) can be very strong. When the physical surroundings (of high ceilings and dim lights) are combined with the ritual sequence (of stand, sing, sit, pray, etc.), it is very easy to be entrapped and to commit the crime of deception and hypocrisy. *We must avoid being carried along through the motions of worship by our environment.*

Third, our environment can provide the needed input for the response of worship. If we are reading a good theology book, or if we are listening to a friend tell about the Lord's faithfulness in his life, we are receiving input for worship. In this sense, an atmosphere for worship has been created. So, we can conclude that there *is* such a thing as an atmosphere of worship. At times this atmosphere is helpful; at times it is dangerous.

Yet there is another sense in which worship is so highly *personal* that the atmosphere should make little difference. God's worth can be consciously expressed on a busy highway, or in a committee meeting. Of course, there are some environments which are so distracting that thought about God is difficult, such as when we are watching a slam-bam car chase on TV. But there is a deeper sense in which we can neither *depend* on our environment to cause us to worship, nor *blame* our environment if we fail to worship. With this in mind, the concept of an atmosphere of worship loses much of its significance.

The person who is responsible for planning worship services should try to remove distractions. Dim lights and rituals should be avoided, lest we program people through some thoughtless motions of worship. And, most importantly, plenty of information about God should be provided as input for worship.

Remember, when we are in a traditional worship setting, we shouldn't just go through the motions. Instead, we should *mean what we express.* Nor do we wait for the weekly, traditional worship setting in order to worship. If we know something good about God, we should express it to God, silently, verbally, or by our actions.

"The true worshipers will worship the Father in spirit and truth; for they are the kind of worshipers the Father seeks" (John 4:23).

MUSIC AS A METHOD OF INSTRUCTION

 PRINCIPLE 29: Music has a significant place in Christian ministry as a method of conveying a message. The words are the most important part of a song.

Music in the church is a touchy subject. Miss A is jealous of Miss B's singing ability. Mrs. C is offended by Mr. D's music. E, F, and G don't like the choir leader's selections. H always asks for the same song during Sunday evening "favorites." I, J, K, L, M, N, and O don't like being told to smile when the congregation sings "What a Friend We Have in Jesus." P (the pastor) always sings off key. Q thinks that R is just showing off by hitting those high notes at the end of the song. S and T think the congregation should always sing all the stanzas of each song. U thinks the children's choir should sing more often. V and W think the ladies' trio should sing less often. X sings too loud in the alto section of the choir. And Y and Z think the electric bass belongs in the night club, not in the church. Everyone has a musical complaint because everyone is focusing his attention on the style rather than on the message of the songs.

THE IMPORTANCE OF THE WORDS

The distinction between style and message is the single most important distinction we can make in analyzing church music. "Style" refers to musical aspects such as notes, rhythm, melody, harmony, tone, dynamics, arrangement, tempo, and accompaniment. "Message" refers to the lyrics of the song, that is, the ideas and the teachings contained in the words. If we paid less attention to style and more attention to message, most of the above complaints would disappear.

The Bible repeatedly emphasizes the words of a song rather than the style. Paul told the Ephesian believers to "*speak* to one another with psalms, hymns and spiritual songs" (Eph. 5:19) and the Colossian believers to "let the word of Christ dwell in you richly as you teach and admonish one another with all wisdom, and as you sing psalms, hymns and spiritual songs" (Col 3:16). Notice that the commands are not primarily commands to sing, but to convey a message. The content of the message is referred to as "the word of Christ." Communicating the message is the central thing; the singing is merely the method. (And, of course, it is only one of several methods of conveying a message.)

Paul also implied the importance of the words of a song when he said, "I will sing with my spirit, but I will also sing with my mind" (1 Cor. 14:15). In the context Paul was stressing the importance of intelligible communication with others. One of the books of the Bible serves as a testimony to the importance of the words. The lyrics of the hymns that ancient Israel used to sing are preserved for us in the book of Psalms; the melodies, however, are lost.

A good song is a song that does an effective job of communicating a message. The message should, of course, be biblically sound. Lyrics should be either straight from the Bible, based on a Bible passage, or in harmony with the teachings of the Bible. (Traditionally, songs containing words addressed to God have been called hymns, while songs containing words addressed to other people have been called gospel songs.)

This emphasis on the importance of the words does not mean that the style of a song is unimportant. The style should help convey the general spirit or feeling of the words. Somber words should be set to somber music. Happy words should be set to cheery or upbeat music. Words of majesty should be accompanied by majestic sounds. Words of prayer should be set in a quiet style. And words of warfare should be set in a militant style. The style should always support the words rather than drawing attention to itself.

THE USE AND MISUSE OF MUSIC

Unfortunately, many pastors and song leaders have a low view of the place of music in the meetings of the church. Often the music is chosen only for its style and not for its words. A quiet song is chosen to "set the mood" for the sermon. A four-minute song is chosen to allow enough time for the offering to be taken. A jumpy song is chosen to get the wiggles out of the kids. But music is more than a mere time filler, or entertainment, or a means of transition between the "important parts" of the program. Music preaches. Music teaches. Music exhorts. Music comforts. In short, music ministers!

The song leader can do a lot to insure that music is used properly in your church. He can select songs with words that relate well to the pastor's message. The words might emphasize one of the points of the message, or they might provide an appropriate response to the message. When he introduces the songs he can draw attention to the words in various ways. He can ask the congregation a question that is answered by the words of the song. He can tell them about the author or the circumstances in which the words were written. He can ask the congregation to compare the words with certain Scripture passages. Or he can even stop in the middle of a song and ask the congregation to discuss what they think a certain phrase means. And, of course, he should avoid anything which draws attention away from the words of the song. For example, he should avoid telling the congregation to sing louder. Good singing has to do with the activity of the mind, not the force of the lungs. It may be distracting to ask the women to sing one stanza and the men the next. He should avoid over-directing a song. When he leads songs, he should think of himself, not as a Toscanini but as a teacher with an important idea to be communicated.

The question of whether rock music should be used in church has created controversy, mainly because the focus has been on the style rather than the message. The conflict could be greatly eased if both those listening and those performing would keep the words in the forefront. Listeners should remember not to evaluate a song by its style primarily, but by its message. They should also learn to exercise reasonable tolerance of musical styles they don't like just as they must exercise reasonable tolerance of various hair styles, clothing styles, and even preaching styles. Those who sing and play in church should remember to select their songs on the basis of the lyrics. They should also remember that whether or not the style of the music hinders the communication of the message depends upon the listeners' backgrounds and preferences. If the rock idiom offends your listeners, the message will not get through. If your listeners are comfortable with the rock idiom, then it can be used to convey the message.

Whatever the style, music can be a powerful tool of instruction. It can be used effectively with children, youth, and adults. It can be used both for evangelism and for edification. We should not underestimate either the benefits that can come from the proper use of music or the problems that can come from the misuse of music.

ELDERS (PASTORS)

 PRINCIPLE 30: Every local church should have a group of qualified elders (pastors) as the main teachers and disciplers of adults.

There are two offices, or positions of leadership, in the local church: elder and deacon. We will begin by examining the office of elder.

ELDER, BISHOP, OVERSEER, SHEPHERD, PASTOR

The terms elder, bishop, overseer, shepherd, and pastor all refer to the same office in the local church. This can be seen by examining the Greek words that are used in the New Testament to refer to church leaders. The word *presbuteros,* which is used over sixty times in the New Testament, means an aged person or elder. The word *episkopos* means overseer or superintendent and is also translated "bishop" in some translations. The word *poimen* means shepherd and is translated "pastor" in one passage (Eph. 4:11).

These three Greek words are used interchangeably in several passages. In Acts 20 we read that "Paul sent to Ephesus for the *elders* of the church" (v. 17). Later, Paul told them, "Guard yourselves and all the flock of which the Holy Spirit has made you overseers. Be shepherds of the church of God" (v. 28). Thus, *presbuteros, episkopos,* and *poimen* were all used to refer to the same group of leaders from the church of Ephesus. In Titus 1:5-7 the church leader is called both elder *(presbuteros)* and overseer *(episkopos).* And in 1 Peter 5:1 and 2 elders *(presbuteros)* were told to be shepherds *(poimen).*

Thus, there are three Greek words which the writers of the New Testament used interchangeably to refer to the official spiritual leaders of the local church. These three Greek words are translated into five English words which we can also use interchangeably to refer to our church leaders: elder, bishop, overseer, shepherd, and pastor. Note that the word deacon *(diakonos)* is not used in any of these passages. The office of deacon is a different office.

PLURALITY OF ELDERS IN EACH LOCAL CHURCH

Paul and Barnabas appointed, or held elections for, elders (note the plural) in each church they had established in Lystra, Iconium, and Antioch (Acts 14:23). There was a plurality of elders in the church at Jerusalem (Acts 15:2-4), at Ephesus (Acts 20:17), and at Philippi (Phil. 1:1). Titus was told by Paul to appoint elders in every town on the island of Crete (Titus 1:5). James instructed the believer to call for the elders of the church when he was sick (James 5:14). And Paul spoke of several who were "over" the Thessalonians (1 Thess. 5:12; compare Heb. 13:17). Having a plurality of elders was standard practice in the local churches of the New Testament.

Some maintain the view that each church should have only one pastor by claiming that there are two kinds of elders, teaching elders and ruling elders. According to this idea, which is supposedly based on 1 Timothy 5:17, each church would have one teaching elder and he would be called the pastor. Each church would also have a plurality of ruling elders who would be below the pastor's position in authority. But this view is not well supported in Scripture; 1 Timothy 5:17 does not even hint that there should be only one teaching elder in each church, or that (if there were only one) he should rule over the other elders. Also, in light of what Jesus told his disciples about the insignificance of position (Matt. 20:25-28; 23:6-12) it would be strange indeed if Paul had told Timothy to reward certain elders just because of their position (as though 1 Timothy 5:17 established the teaching and preaching elders as a distinct group who were especially deserving of double honor). Furthermore, since there is only one set of qualifications for elders, and since all elders must be apt to teach, we conclude that there is really only one kind of elder.

There is no term of office given in the New Testament for the elders. Evidently, they were to remain elders as long as they wanted to and as long as they continued to meet the qualifications.

In many conservative and evangelical churches today there is only one pastor. According to this practice the pastor is often above the other church leaders (whether they are called elders or deacons or whatever) and he is the only one who is referred to as the minister. He ministers while the others sit on the board and make policy decisions. There are four serious problems created by this practice. First, it does not square with Scripture. Second, it tends to give too much power to one person. Third, it expects too much ministry from one person. Fourth, it robs the others of the chance to minister. All of these problems are solved when the church has a plurality of pastors or elders. This does not mean, however, that it is improper for one elder among the several to have extended formal training or to devote full time to the work. The danger, though, is in viewing this one as the only one who ministers or viewing him above the others when it comes to making decisions.

There is a great deal of wisdom in having more than one elder (pastor) in each local church. By having several, the burden of the ministry is not overwhelming on any one person. Also, each elder has different gifts and abilities and is able to relate better to certain individuals than others. So, each person in the church is more likely to have a satisfying relationship with a pastor. And, of course, the collective insight and wisdom of several people will be more balanced than that of one individual.

QUALIFICATIONS OF THE ELDERS

Elders must be "above reproach" (1 Tim. 3:2) or "blameless" (Titus 1:6, 7). This was the first qualification mentioned in both of Paul's lists of qualifications for elders. Of course, this was not a reference to sinless perfection. Rather, it was an emphasis on the importance of the character and life of the church leader.

Paul gave both Timothy and Titus specific, detailed instructions regarding the qualifications for elders (see the chart below). Note that these lists say nothing about the individual's ability to address large groups with forceful eloquence, to organize and administer an efficient church organization, to promote successfully the various programs of the church, or to raise funds. Nor do they say anything about his formal training.

1 Timothy 3:1-7 — Titus 1:5-9
ABOVE REPROACH — BLAMELESS

The husband of but one wife —	The husband of but one wife
Temperate; self-controlled, —	Not overbearing; not quick
Not violent but gentle;	tempered; not violent; self-
Not quarrelsome	controlled; disciplined

1 Timothy 3:1-7	Titus 1:5-9
Hospitable	Hospitable
Able to teach	Hold firmly to the trustworthy message as it has been taught so that he can encourage others by sound doctrine and refute those who oppose it
Not given to much wine	Not given to much wine
Not a lover of money	Not pursuing dishonest gain
Manage his own family well and see that his children obey him with proper respect	A man whose children believe and are not open to the charge of being wild and disobedient
Not a recent convert	One who loves what is good
Respectable; a good reputation with outsiders	Upright; holy

These qualifications can be summarized under six categories: (1) how long he has been a Christian, (2) personality traits which reflect the fruit of the Spirit, (3) fidelity in marriage and success with his family, (4) knowledge of the Bible and ability to teach, (5) reputation, and (6) freedom from vices.

Because of the educational level of our North American culture he should also have formal training. Such training can contribute a great deal to the fourth category given above. However, churches make a serious mistake if they look for such qualifications as formal training and speaking and administrative abilities but forget about all the other matters of Christian character which were listed by Paul.

Many of these qualifications, especially those in categories 2, 3, 5, and 6, are rather difficult for a congregation to find out about unless they know the individual personally. Many times a congregation never learns about these personal matters because they are considering a pastor from another location. They do not have enough time to get to know him and his family well or to find out about his character and reputation.

If they were selecting an elder (pastor) from among their own congregation they would already know him quite well. Also, he would know them quite well. He would not have to spend the first year getting acquainted with the people of the church. Unfortunately, many churches never think about looking among their own members for elders. They fall into the trap of believing that pastors are always hired from far away. The New Testament churches grew their own leadership.

DUTIES OF ELDERS

While Paul gave Timothy and Titus very explicit teaching in two extended sections of his letters regarding the qualifications of elders, he did not do the same for the elders' duties. The reason was simple. If we have the proper Christian character, we will not need a list of duties to follow. In other words, if we have the "right stuff," we will know what needs to be done. How dangerous it would have been for Paul to have supplied a long list of duties but to have said nothing about the qualifications. Instead, he stressed the qualifications and made only incidental references to the duties of the elders. We can put these incidental references together with a few other lines of evidence from the New Testament and come up with some general statements about the duties of elders. The words themselves imply some areas of responsibility.

The word "elder" suggests the ability to apply wisdom to the situations and needs of the church. An overseer, is one who oversees or superintends, who has an overall perspective on the life and work of the church. A shepherd is one who feeds, cares for, and guards the flock.

The New Testament concept of leadership (Luke 22:24-27; Matt. 20:25-28; 23:6-12) requires the elder to see himself as a servant of others, "not lording it over those entrusted to [them], but being examples to the flock" (1 Pet. 5:3).

Besides these, we have Jesus' own example of humble service and sacrifice (Phil. 2:3-8; Eph. 5:25; John 13:12-17) and Paul's own example of personal caring (1 Thess. 2:7, 8, 11). When Paul referred to the elder as one who would *take care* of God's church" (1 Tim. 3:5), he used the same Greek word that Luke used to describe the way the good Samaritan took care of the roadside victim (Luke 10:33-35). Certainly this was a personal, compassionate kind of caring.

So, we are not without some general ideas of the attitudes and activities of the elder. Besides this, we have such duties mentioned as directing the affairs of the church, working hard in word and teaching, encouraging, refuting, shepherding, being examples, and praying (1 Tim. 3:5; 5:17; Titus 1:9; Acts 20:28; 1 Pet. 5:3; James 5:14).

But what are the elder's *most important* responsibilities? Two passages explicitly place certain duties in priority above others. In Acts 6:1-4 we read that the apostles (who functioned as the first elders) gave their attention to the *ministry of the word* and *prayer* rather than distributing food to widows. In 1 Timothy 5:17 those who *work hard in word* and *teach* are singled out as especially noteworthy among those who direct the affairs of the church. (The *New International Version* says "preaching," but the literal rendering is "in word.") And it is certainly no accident that "pastors" and "teachers" are closely related, perhaps even identified with each other, in Ephesians 4:11. Thus, the ministry of the word (which is probably essentially the same as teaching and working hard in word) and prayer emerge as the elder's two principal responsibilities.

The following chart summarizes the work of the elder and contrasts it with the popular view of the elder or pastor that is held in many of our churches today. The popular view of the work of the elder appears to be borrowed from the business world rather than from the New Testament. It does not adequately emphasize either the central concept of the elder's work (serving people) or the priority duties of the elder (prayer and teaching). *The biblical concept of the work of the elder requires that he have intensive and extensive interaction with people.* The popular view does not.

Thus, our churches today have a dual problem when it comes to leadership. First, many church leaders are simply not qualified to be elders. Second, the current notion of what an elder is and what his duties are does not square with the New Testament. Churches cannot be expected to rise above their leaders, so we should not be surprised at the sad state of many churches in view of the sad state of the leadership.

NEW TESTAMENT VIEW

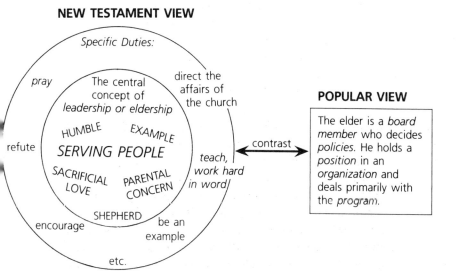

Should an elder (pastor) be called a preacher? Regrettably, "pastor" and "preacher" are considered synonymous by many. The word "preach" is often equated with sermonizing or teaching doctrine to believers. However, in the New Testament, "preach" is used mainly to refer to the proclamation of the gospel to nonbelievers. Certainly any pastor should preach (evangelize) when he has opportunity to do so with non-Christians, but his responsibilities *toward believers* do not include preaching (evangelism).

If we think about the biblical view of the elder, we will recognize that the work of the elder is the work of disciple making. Even though the terminology is not identical, the basic ministry is. The elders are the principal disciple makers in the church. Certainly parents are the main disciplers of their own children, but we should expect the elders in the local church to be regularly discipling the adults.

DEACONS

The office of deacon *(diakonos)* is a different office than that of the elder. The word *diakonos* is a general word which means "minister" or "servant." Even though all Christians are to serve and minister to others, some Christians are recognized and approved by a local church as servants and are given responsibility for specific duties. These recognized servants are the deacons.

The duties of deacons can include any area of general service (as distinguished from the spiritual leadership of the church, which is the responsibility of the elders). As needs arise, deacons can be appointed to meet those needs. According to the pattern in the New Testament, every local church should have elders, but not every church needs deacons.

The qualifications for deacons, like the qualifications

for elders, focus on the character of the individual (Acts 6:3; 1 Tim. 3:8-13). Both men and women can be officially approved deacons. Qualifications for both men and women deacons are given in 1 Timothy 3:8-13, and Phoebe is named as a servant (deacon) of the church in Cenchrea (Rom. 16:1). The qualifications for deacons are quite similar to the qualifications for elders, but there are some significant differences. Elders must be able to teach, but this qualification is not listed for the deacons. Evidently, elders are the main teachers in the local church, not the deacons. Also, since deacons are selected for specific duties as the needs arise, and since the office of deacon is not a universal one nor a permanent one, deacons are not expected to rule, as are the elders. The sphere of authority of the deacon is limited to the area of the need that has arisen.

NINE
ORGANIZATION, THE FORMAL STRUCTURE OF CHRISTIAN MINISTRY

PRINCIPLE 31
Planning and Evaluation

PRINCIPLE 32
Departmentalization and Agencies

PRINCIPLE 33
Curriculum Materials

PLANNING AND EVALUATION

 PRINCIPLE **31: Proper planning begins with evaluation, is based on clear goals, and ends with evaluation.**

Proper planning occurs in a cycle, as illustrated below. This planning and evaluation cycle is also known as the "educational cycle."

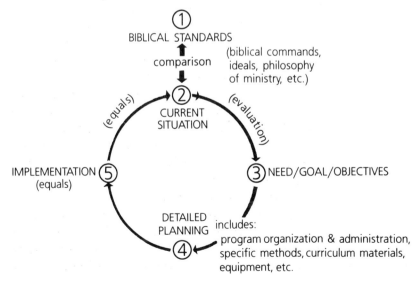

This cycle will not work properly unless the person doing the planning has two things in his background. First, he must be familiar with the Bible's standards, its philosophy of ministry, its ideals, and its commands. Second, he must have had months of personal experience within the situation so that he is very familiar with the people, the programs, and the organization.

A person who comes into a situation as a leader often begins too quickly to make plans to change things. He may have an excellent grasp of the biblical standards, but he does not yet know enough about the situation to make wise plans. Or, the opposite may be the case. The person who has been in the situation for a long time may make plans based on his personal preferences or on the way other groups do things. He may know the present situation well, but he cannot evaluate it properly without a good understanding of the biblical standards.

In order to make good plans, one must have *both* of these things in his background, a grasp of the biblical standards and personal familiarity with the situation.

PROPER PLANNING BEGINS WITH EVALUATION

In making plans for a program, organization, meeting, or activity (whether it is a new one or an existing one that ought to be changed), the first thing we should do is to evaluate the current situation in light of the biblical standards and thus identify the need. When we compare the current situation with the biblical standards we will soon see where it falls short. This comparison, or evaluation, is crucial. It is the only way to identify the true need. Any time we try to make plans without having this true need clearly in mind, our plans are entirely beside the point. If our planning is not aimed at meeting the need, why plan?

PROPER PLANNING IS BASED ON CLEAR GOALS

When we have identified the need, we have, by doing so, established a goal. After all, a statement of need is the negative side of the coin; it indicates what should be the case but isn't. The goal is the positive side of the same coin; it is a statement of what we hope will be the case after we have implemented our plans.

Perhaps our goal is clear to us, but not specific and concrete enough to help us make any actual plans. If so, we should spell out several specific and achievable objectives which, when put together, will satisfy our general goal. Often it is wise to set deadlines for accomplishing each of these objectives, especially if they involve a sequence of steps, some of which must be completed before others can be started.

Once we have spelled out specific and concrete goals or objectives, we can plan all the various details, which might include schedules of meetings, choice of curriculum materials, a list of topics for discussion, selecting the location of activities, selection of the people who will be the leaders, the listing of duties of officers, selection of specific methods, the matching of gifted individuals with certain responsibilities, determination of the communication procedures, the decision as to what records to keep, the estimating of expenditures and sources of income, or any of a thousand other details. However, it is very important to plan each detail with the goal and objectives clearly in mind. When we get wrapped up in the details, we can easily forget the reason for all the planning, or what we had hoped to accomplish. When we are making our detailed plans, we must keep the goal and objectives in front of us.

PROPER PLANNING ENDS WITH EVALUATION

After the plans are implemented and the new program or organization has been functioning for awhile, its success should be evaluated. When we make the evaluation the basic question to ask is, How well does it satisfy the need that was identified at the start? At the same time, of course, we are comparing the new situation with the biblical standards to see if any new needs come to light. Thus, this evaluation-needs-planning-implementation-evaluation cycle is an ongoing process. The cycle should be repeated over and over again.

The Bible and its commands, ideals, and philosophy of ministry must always be the basis for the comparison. Success is determined by how well our programs and organizations carry out the biblical standards, not by how large the meetings are, how large the budget is, how fancy the building is, or how it compares with what other groups are doing.

AN EXAMPLE
(The numbers in front of the paragraphs below correspond to the numbers in the preceding diagram.)

1. One of the biblical standards is that parents have the primary responsibility for the Christian nurture of their children.

2. However, the current situation in many homes and churches is that the church's schedule is too full. Family members spend very little time interacting with each other. In fact, they may be so out of practice that they have forgotten how. If they were given the time to interact, perhaps all they would know how to do would be to watch the television "together."

3. By comparing the current situation with the biblical ideal, the need becomes obvious. Parents need more time with each other and with their children. They probably also need motivation and practical instruction on their responsibilities and how to carry them out. Specific objectives might include:

a. A cluster program in which several of the former week-night meetings are rescheduled to meet on the same evening (perhaps Wednesday). This would allow each family to come together to church and leave together, instead of each family member having to leave home on a different night of the week.

b. Instruction of parents regarding their responsibilities and how to carry them out. This might be done through the pastor's sermons, Sunday school classes, etc.

c. Election of elders who are family oriented. These would be elders who have been successful family men themselves, who are able to give wise counsel to other families, and who are sensitive to the needs of families and can guide the development of the overall church program so that it enhances the ministry of parents rather than detracting from it.

4. Many specific details would need to be planned to meet each of the objectives suggested above. Of course, it is impossible to spell out all of these details here because they would depend on the unique circumstances, people, and resources in each church or community. Again, it should be stated how easily one forgets the main objectives as one gets involved in the fine details of planning. We would be wise to spell out the goal and objectives *in writing* and to keep them before us so that we can remind ourselves of them often during the planning process.

5. The implementation of our plans then becomes the new (current) situation which should be evaluated in light of the original goal and objectives (and ultimately in light of the biblical standards).

DEPARTMENTALIZATION AND AGENCIES

 PRINCIPLE 32: The ministry of the local church is divided into a variety of agencies serving various age groups. Each agency is designed to meet particular needs.

DEPARTMENTALIZATION

The typical church is made up of a complex array of individuals of varying ages, different backgrounds, and unique spiritual needs. If the church tried to minister to all these people with just one agency or one type of meeting, many needs would probably not be met. Through division and specialization, the church can provide a ministry that will be meaningful and helpful to such a heterogeneous group.

The following chart shows some typical agencies along with the ages to which they minister and the elements, or activities, they usually provide. Of course, the names for the various departments and agencies vary widely from church to church. The size of the church sometimes determines whether some of these

SOME OF THE ELEMENTS (ACTIVITIES) IN THE LIFE OF THE CHURCH	Family	Worship Serv.	Sunday School	Child. Church	Evening Serv.	Prayer Meeting	Youth Group	Clubs	Graded Choir
Evangelism	XXX		X					X	
Instruction	XXX	X	X	X	X	X	X	X	X
Worship	XXX	X		X					
Fellowship	XXX		X		X	X	X		
Prayer	XXX					X			
Service	XXX								X

DIVISION	DEPARTMENT	AGE or GRADE	Family	Worship Serv.	Sunday School	Child. Church	Evening Serv.	Prayer Meeting	Youth Group	Clubs	Graded Choir
Adult ages 22 & up	Senior Adult	60 & up		X	X		X	X			X
	Middle Adult	35/40-60		X	X		X	X			X
	Young Adult	22-35/40		X	X		X	X			X
Youth ages 12-21	Collge-Career	college age		X	X		X	X	X		X
	High School	grade 10-12	X	X	X		X	X	X	X	X
	Junior High	grade 7-9	X	X	X		X	X	X	X	X
Children ages 0-11	Junior	grade 5-6	X		X	X		(X)		X	X
	Middler	grade 3-4	X		X	X		(X)		X	X
	Primary	grade 1-2	X		X	X		(X)			X
	Beginner	age 4-5	X		X	X		(X)			
	Nursery	age 2-3	X		X	X		(X)			
	Cradle Roll & Toddler	up to 24 mo.	X		X	X		(X)			

agencies are feasible. This chart is not meant to show the "right" way to organize the ministry of the local church as if there were only one way to do it. In any given church there could be several effective ways to divide the ages and agencies. This chart is meant to show one way it *is* being done, not necessarily the way it should be done.

Notice that the younger ages are more closely graded than the older ages. In the children's division, the departments cover only two years each, while in the adult division the departments cover many years. The departments for younger ages are more closely graded because children's abilities and needs change much more rapidly than adults'. A four-year-old is remarkably different than a two-year-old, and this difference is largely due to the rapid development that takes place over the two-year span. But a thirty-four-year-old is much the same as he was two years earlier.

In five of the departments (primary through high school) a person's school grade, rather than his age, determines what department he is in. This makes it more likely that school friends will be together and that reading level and class participation skills will be similar.

Nine agencies are listed at the top of the chart. Of course, any of the elements can be found at times in any of the agencies. Each different agency is specifically intended to meet certain types of needs and thus to emphasize certain elements. The "x's" in the top part of the chart indicate only the elements which each agency emphasizes.

Notice that the family is listed first among these agencies. Unfortunately, the family is often the most neglected agency in church planning. Since the family was established long before the church, it is not "designed" to meet specific needs in the same sense as the other specialized agencies. Yet it can be more influential than all the other agencies combined. The triple "x's" under the family are there to remind us that family life should include all these elements, and that it can do so in a very effective manner because of the personal, informal, and extended nature of its ministry.

Notice that all of the agencies include the element of instruction. Instruction, as discussed under Principle 27, is the most basic of all the elements and should be an important activity of every church agency.

Notice that the Sunday school is typically the only agency which is geared to minister to all age groups. Notice also that there are more agencies designed to meet the needs of those in junior high and high school than any other age group.

By dividing up different ages, and by designing the various agencies to include different elements, the church is able to minister to a wide variety of individuals and their unique spiritual needs. But such division and specialization is not all that can be done.

ELECTIVES

Adults and older youth are usually fairly realistic about their needs. A child will typically ask for what he wants, but more mature individuals are more likely to ask for what they need, so it is often wise to let older youth and adults choose for themselves what topics they will study. For example, the Sunday school might offer several classes on different subjects and then allow each adult to elect which class he will attend. Even if the adult Sunday school classes remain organized according to age, at least the members in each class can be given some choice in selecting the subject to be studied.

If electives are offered continually, the social ties that have been built up over the years may begin to break down. In order to maintain these healthy social ties, the Sunday school can organize its adults by age for two quarters of the year, and by interest (electives) for the other two quarters. Age-group socials can even be planned during the quarters when electives are being offered.

Both children and adults need certain things and want certain things. What children need and what they want do not coincide very often. So the leader will have to make sure that needs and wants are balanced. However, what adults need and what they want should coincide more often. So when the leaders let the adults choose, the adults will often get both what they want and what they need.

CURRICULUM MATERIALS

 PRINCIPLE **33: Curriculum materials can be of great value to a local church, but they must be chosen carefully and adapted to local needs.**

The word "curriculum" is actually very broad in its meaning. It includes all different types of learning experiences for the student whether or not any printed materials are used in those learning experiences. Here we are concerned mainly with printed curriculum materials, those materials put out by the various denominational and nondenominational publishers.

VALUES AND LIMITATIONS
OF CURRICULUM MATERIALS

The use of published curriculum materials can have great value for a local church. Those who write the materials usually know their Bibles *and* know people and how they learn. Those who write curriculum materials for children are usually well acquainted with child psychology and have had considerable experience working with children. The publishers usually have a systematic plan worked out so that they cover a wide range of important Bible passages and topics over a given period of time.

However, there is one thing publishers cannot know, and that is *our class*. Publishers gear their materials to average abilities and typical needs. No matter what publisher's materials we use, *we will have to adapt the materials* to the particular group we are teaching. Sometimes we will get only an idea from the materials. Occasionally we will be able to use a whole lesson as it is written. But we should not expect to follow the materials week after week without making many adjustments for our unique learners. By gearing the lesson to the specific needs of our unique class we will be "building others up *according to their needs*" (Eph. 4:29).

STRUCTURE OF THE CURRICULUM

Curriculum publishers follow one of several patterns throughout their program. Lessons are either correlated to the uniform lesson series or the material may be geared to what they perceive to be the unique needs and abilities of people on each of the graded levels. Although these two options are not completely mutually exclusive, they do work against each other. For example, a lesson which is completely geared to the unique needs and abilities of a fifth grader will not do a very good job of meeting the needs of a college age student, making it difficult to correlate the lessons for these two ages. However, there are some common needs and common themes which can be correlated among all ages. Also, the same *basic* lesson can be taught to different ages as long as the manner in which it is taught and the methods that are used are geared to the unique abilities of each different age. So even though the two options pull in

different directions, publishers do not have to choose one
option and forget the other option altogether.

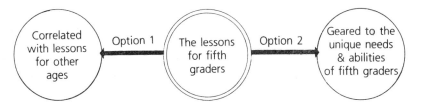

The advantage of the first option is that the
department superintendent will find it easier to have a
common theme for worship. Also, families may find it
easier to discuss their similar lessons. The advantage of
the second option is that the learner will probably find
the lessons more interesting, relevant to his needs, and
understandable. Of these two advantages, the second
advantage seems to be more crucial than the first
because the second advantage is a prerequisite to the
first. Only when the lesson is relevant and understood by
the learner will he be able to make meaningful
connections between the lesson and the departmental
worship experience or to discuss it with his family.

Different publishers have attacked this problem in
different ways. The categories listed below represent
some of their solutions to the problem.

Uniform materials: All ages have the same lesson based
on the same Scripture passage. This solution is based on
the first option. (e.g.: Union Gospel Press)

Unified materials: Various departments have different
lessons, but they are all based on the same theme. This
solution attempts to combine the two options. (e.g.: David
C. Cook)

Departmentally graded materials: All classes within a
department have the same lesson, but it is different from

the lesson in other departments. This solution attempts to combine the two options, favoring the second option. (e.g.: Scripture Press)

Closely graded materials: Each age or grade has a different lesson. This solution is based on the second option. (e.g.: Gospel Light)

EVALUATING AND CHOOSING YOUR CURRICULUM MATERIALS

Most churchgoers have a definite opinion about the curriculum materials their church uses. However, these opinions are seldom based on a thorough evaluation of the materials. Instead, such opinions are often the result of one-factor analysis. For example, a teacher doesn't like her materials because the questions seem too hard for her students. A member of a young adult class might wish the Scripture passages were all printed out in his book so he wouldn't have to keep flipping back and forth in his Bible. A department superintendent may want to find a better curriculum because his does not tell him what to do with the first fifteen minutes of Sunday school.

Often a church will base its choice of a curriculum on such opinions about isolated factors. This way of choosing gives rise to a fairly common phenomenon in our local churches of adopting a new curriculum about every other year. The new curriculum is chosen to satisfy those who complained. But other folks become dissatisfied with the new curriculum and that curriculum is also soon discarded.

Of course, everyone is entitled to his personal preferences. But who needs a biennial curriculum change? Each church does need to thoroughly analyze several curriculums in light of several important factors. The curriculum evaluation form that follows this section analyzes these aspects:

1. Doctrine
2. Use of the Bible
3. Salvation and Christian Growth
4. Teaching Aims
5. The Teacher
6. The Learning Process
7. Organization of the Material

When several curriculums are evaluated and compared, we will notice that each one is strong in certain areas and weak in others. We will have to decide which areas are most important for us. Most churches make the area of doctrine the key area of evaluation, and rightly so. However, we shouldn't make doctrine our *sole* area of evaluation. We shouldn't be satisfied just to have a curriculum that is doctrinally sound. We should find one that is also balanced in emphasis and educationally sound.

Who should do the evaluation? As a general guideline, the pastors and enough people to have a representative cross section of those who will end up using the chosen curriculum should be included in the decision-making process. Care should be taken not to include so many people that the process becomes cumbersome.

Whatever curriculum is adopted, the group should remember that no curriculum will fit every situation perfectly. Each local church will have to *adapt* whatever curriculum it chooses. The choice should be based on the overall evaluation of all the factors included in the following form. Then, when individuals find these things in the curriculum that they don't like, they should adjust the curriculum materials to their own unique situation and to their own personal liking.

One more basic idea is often overlooked in curriculum evaluation. Every effort should be made to understand the curriculum's philosophy, its overall purpose and approach. This understanding will help teachers grasp the significance of certain features of the curriculum that otherwise might seem incidental. Even though there are several items in the evaluation form which relate to the curriculum's philosophy, one will often have to look further to find a clear statement of philosophy.

Many publishers include a preface in their teacher's materials which explains their philosophy. Some publishers supply a separate prospectus or introductory booklet that explains their strategy or gives an overview of their curriculum. And some will even be glad to send a representative to explain their materials and their philosophy.

Some final suggestions might be kept in mind as the evaluation form is used. Instead of reading the first item on the form and then paging through the curriculum materials to find the answer, the complete evaluation form should be studied, the materials skimmed, and then, starting with the first item on the form, the appropriate number should be circled and then brief but specific comments should be made to explain the evaluation. Comparisons can be made quite easily if the evaluation of two different curriculums are written out on the same form, using different colored pens.

CURRICULUM EVALUATION FORM

Publisher _____

Denomination (if not independent)   _____

Department or age of grade (if
this is a limited evaluation)   _____

Name of person making evaluation   _____

Date of evaluation _____

	Don't know, or irrelevant	Strongly disagree	Disagree	Neutral	Agree	Strongly agree	Comments

A. DOCTRINE

1. The curriculum presents the *Bible as the authoritative and accurate Word of God,* fully inspired and fully reliable.

    x   1 2 3 4 5

2. The curriculum teaches that *God is* there. (He exists in objective reality, and he is spiritual, personal, and triune.)

    x   1 2 3 4 5

3. The curriculum teaches that *man was created perfect by God,* but he *fell* into sin so that *now all persons are sinners* under God's punishment, now and eternally.

    x   1 2 3 4 5

4. The curriculum teaches that *Jesus Christ is both God and man,* that he took our punishment by *dying for our sins,* and that he is *physically alive today.*

    x   1 2 3 4 5

5. The curriculum teaches that *faith (trust) in the person and work of Jesus Christ* is necessary and sufficient for one's salvation, now and eternally.

    x   1 2 3 4 5

B. USE OF THE BIBLE

6. Stress is placed on *biblical basics* (such as the above five doctrines) rather than on secondary issues.

    x   1 2 3 4 5

7. The *entire Bible* is "covered" (some portions in greater detail than others, of course).

    x   1 2 3 4 5

	Don't know, or irrelevant	Strongly disagree	Disagree	Neutral	Agree	Strongly agree	Comments

8. The learner is helped to *organize, and interrelate* various aspects of his doctrinal beliefs and Bible knowledge rather than leaving all facts and principles in isolation.

   x   1 2 3 4 5

9. *Extrabiblical materials* (stories, illustrations, etc.) *support* the teachings and emphases of the Bible.

   x   1 2 3 4 5

10. All the *lessons are clearly taken from the Bible* or are clearly related to the Bible. (There are many references to and quotations from the Bible, and many in-depth studies of key Bible passages.)

   x   1 2 3 4 5

11. Both teacher and learner are encouraged to *go directly to the Bible* and discover its teachings inductively, both in class and out of class. The Bible is used more than the teacher's manual and the learners' books.

   x   1 2 3 4 5

C. SALVATION AND CHRISTIAN GROWTH

12. *The Gospel* (the plan of salvation) *is presented clearly and repeatedly,* especially in the primary and junior lessons.

   x   1 2 3 4 5

13. *Christian growth is stressed* for those who are already saved. Many *practical areas of Christian living,* including witnessing, interpersonal relationships, family living, missions, etc., are dealt with throughout the youth and adult lessons.

   x   1 2 3 4 5

D. TEACHING AIMS

	Don't know, or irrelevant	Strongly disagree	Disagree	Neutral	Agree	Strongly agree	Comments
14. *Aims* are clearly stated in the teacher's manual, and are *often focused on learner-action* (actual *use* of the lesson in the learner's life) rather than mere knowledge.	x	1	2	3	4	5	
15. *Aims are based on the typical needs* of learners at each given age, and are *very specific,* rather than pious generalities.	x	1	2	3	4	5	
16. *All aspects* of the departmental time and the class time *are relevant to the aim* for the day (handwork, songs, presession activities, etc.).	x	1	2	3	4	5	

E. THE TEACHER

17. The teacher's *spiritual preparation* is stressed, and the teacher is reminded to *pray* for his individual class members by name.	x	1	2	3	4	5	
18. Teachers are encouraged to think of each class member as a *unique individual* (unique background, desires, abilities, needs, etc.).	x	1	2	3	4	5	
19. The teacher's role as a *model* is stressed; teachers are encouraged to *interact with their learners outside of class,* and practical ways of doing so are suggested.	x	1	2	3	4	5	

F. THE LEARNING PROCESS

20. Both the content of lessons and the methods are *geared to the proper age level* (geared to the learners' needs, interests, capabilities, etc.).	x	1	2	3	4	5	

	Don't know, or irrelevant	Strongly disagree	Disagree	Neutral	Agree	Strongly agree	Comments
21. The teacher is encouraged to function as a *guide*, not merely as a dispenser of knowledge.	x	1	2	3	4	5	
22. Learners are guided to become *aware of personal spiritual needs*.	x	1	2	3	4	5	
23. Learners are helped to determine their own *personal life-implications* for each lesson.	x	1	2	3	4	5	
24. Learners are *challenged to think* for themselves and to *decide* for themselves.	x	1	2	3	4	5	
25. *Practical life-problems* are posed for the learner to *discuss and solve*.	x	1	2	3	4	5	
26. Teachers are encouraged to *meet the learner's basic organismic needs* (acceptance, approval, accomplishment, etc.) in practical ways.	x	1	2	3	4	5	
27. Suggestions are given for *involving children's parents* in the reinforcing of the lesson during the week.	x	1	2	3	4	5	
28. Class procedures and methods stimulate the *meaningful involvement of the learner.*	x	1	2	3	4	5	
29. *Questions are often thought-provoking* rather than being all factual.	x	1	2	3	4	5	
30. A wide *variety of methods* are suggested, and colorful *visuals* are supplied or suggested. *Adequate examples and practical illustrations* are also given.	x	1	2	3	4	5	

	Don't know, or irrelevant	Strongly disagree	Disagree	Neutral	Agree	Strongly agree	Comments
31. *Feedback* from the class (questions, comments, opinions, etc.) is encouraged throughout the lesson.	x	1	2	3	4	5	
32. *Bible memorization* that focuses on the meaning and application of the Bible passage (rather than mere rote memorization) is encouraged.	x	1	2	3	4	5	

G. ORGANIZATION OF THE MATERIAL

33. The *teachers' manuals* are clearly *organized* with plenty of *background material* and sound *teaching tips.*	x	1	2	3	4	5	
34. The curriculum structure is *flexible.* It is *easily adapted to meet urgent learner needs and interests.* Allowances are made for *individual learner-differences; alternate plans* are given for large/small classes, for lack of specific equipment, etc.	x	1	2	3	4	5	
35. *Learners' books* are designed to *facilitate carryover* from the previous lesson early in each week, and to *prepare learners* for the coming lesson late in each week.	x	1	2	3	4	5	
36. Materials are *printed clearly and attractively.* Their *organization and layout* is not confusing.	x	1	2	3	4	5	

OTHER ITEMS TO BE EVALUATED	Don't know, or irrelevant	Strongly disagree	Disagree	Neutral	Agree	Strongly agree	Comments
37.	x	1	2	3	4	5	
38.	x	1	2	3	4	5	
39.	x	1	2	3	4	5	
40.	x	1	2	3	4	5	

TEN
CHANGE, THE REVISION OF CHRISTIAN MINISTRY

PRINCIPLE 34
Change in the Local Church

CHANGE
IN THE LOCAL CHURCH

 PRINCIPLE **34: Patterns and methods of ministry need to be changed if they do not encourage the basic ministry principles to operate. But such structural change depends on new understandings and motivations within individuals, which come about through a gradual educational process.**

We become concerned when we see certain changes that could be made to improve the local church's ministry. However, we have several questions:

Is Christianity a religion of change? Or is it changeless?

Is the change we have in mind the *right* change?

How do we help people *want* to change when they typically want to remain the same?

Will the people *support* this proposed change? And will the change last?

How can we help people through the uncomfortable *process* of change?

Is this the right *time* to make this change?

We need to examine the first question closely since it is basic to the others.

IS CHRISTIANITY CHANGELESS?

What is the proper attitude toward change within Christianity? Some folks never want to change anything; others want to change everything. Of course, neither of these extremes is valid. But we can answer this question if we focus on different aspects of Christianity, because some aspects of Christianity should not change, but others should. Let us examine five aspects: (1) our Lord, (2) the Word of God, (3) basic ministry principles, (4) patterns and methods of ministry, and (5) people.

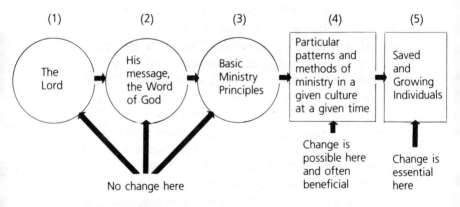

The Lord does not change. He remains constant throughout eternity (James 1:17; Mal. 3:6; Heb. 1:12; 13:8).

The Word of God does not change. Biblical truth cannot be altered; the message of the Bible is the same for all time (1 Pet. 1:25; Matt. 24:35; Ps. 119:89, 160; Isa. 40:8; Gal. 1:6-9).

The basic scriptural principles for Christian ministry do not change. They are principles which are clearly spelled out in Scripture and have universal application. They are to be in operation from church to church, from culture to culture, and from decade to decade.

These three changeless aspects of Christianity, the Lord, the Scripture, and basic ministry principles are explicitly taught in Scripture. An attempt to change these aspects is an attempt to abolish true Christianity. However, just the opposite is the case with the remaining two aspects of Christianity. It will be helpful if we look at the fifth aspect (people) before we look at the fourth (patterns and methods).

Change in people is at the heart of Christianity. Even though the Lord does not change, he desires that people change. Even though the message does not change, it is a life-changing message. Even though the basic ministry principles do not change, they exist for the purpose of effecting change in individuals. In fact, the goal of Christian work *demands* change: both the sudden, positional change of salvation (2 Cor. 5:17), and the gradual, practical change of growth toward Christlikeness (2 Cor. 3:18). These changes are *always* beneficial.

But what about patterns and methods? Whereas basic ministry principles are clearly stated in the Bible, current patterns and methods are not. They are human implementations of the basic ministry principles. Hopefully, but not necessarily, they are also Spirit-led implementations. Since these current patterns and methods are human implementations, they are subject to critical examination and improvement.

Notice that a change in current patterns or methods of ministry does not change the message or the basic ministry principles. For example, particular areas of church and Sunday school *organization* can change; particular aspects of the church's *schedule* and *location* of meetings can change; meeting *format* can change; *financial systems* can change; *equipment* and *teaching aids* can change; but none of these changes necessarily alters the message of the basic ministry principles. In fact, we often notice a wide variation in such patterns and methods from one church to another, from one culture to another, and from one decade to another. Such change *can* be beneficial.

DETERMINING WHEN CHANGE IS NEEDED

We can devise one test to determine when change is needed by relating *patterns and methods* to *basic ministry principles*, and another test by relating *patterns and methods* to *change and growth in individuals*. These two tests, described below, can help you determine whether your church is currently using the best patterns and methods.

The primary test is to find out whether or not the current patterns and methods are allowing *and encouraging* the basic ministry principles to operate. Let's look at an example. A basic ministry principle is: Christians should gather for instruction *and* mutual edification (see Principle 27).

Now let us suppose that in our church there are no meetings which are structured so that the format allows and encourages mutual edification. Instead of having meetings in which believers typically speak up and share things that will edify each other, they are merely encouraged to come and listen. In that case, a change in the current pattern would be beneficial as long as the change brings the current pattern more in line with the basic ministry principle. The key consideration is this: Do the church's current ministry patterns and methods *help* carry out the basic scriptural principles of ministry, or do they hinder them?

The secondary test is to look at the results. If individuals are not becoming saved and are not growing in the Lord, then we may need to change our methods and patterns of ministry. The fault *may* lie elsewhere. There may be an inaccurate or incomplete presentation of the message. Or, the individuals themselves may be willfully unresponsive. But we need to beware of quickly jumping to this last conclusion. It may be more likely that our own patterns and methods are faulty and thus the message and impact never really get through to them so that they *can* respond.

THIRTY-FOUR GUIDELINES FOR MAKING CHANGE

Making change is often very difficult because change is typically contrary to human nature. In fact, how do *we* feel when someone else tries to change us or the way we do things? (The last time this happened to us, was our first reaction one of welcoming the suggestions?) Such changes are even more difficult when old habit patterns are firmly established. How then can we, from within the current situation, stimulate change and at the same time make change *easy* for (or better, *desired* by) our Christian brothers?

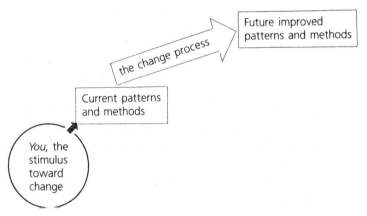

1. *Remember that we are servants of the Lord and of the people as they are.* We shouldn't love them any less just because they presently prefer to do things differently than we would like.

2. *Through an extended educational process we must guide the people to an understanding of the basic scriptural principles of ministry, especially principles concerning their role as Christians who participate in (rather than merely attend) the meetings of the body of Christ.* Believers will respond positively if they see that any patterns or methods we suggest are squarely based on principles from God's Word. This may well require a long educational process within the old patterns before any actual changes are attempted. The pastors' messages are a primary channel for accomplishing this.

3. *We must be patient and gentle and willing to adapt to their pattern for now.* We may feel frustrated when the people evaluate us and our ideas from within their present framework. We may feel that we have to cramp ourselves in order to fit into their mold, but we must do so until we are able to educate them to see things from our (biblical) point of view. Love is patient and gentle (1 Cor. 13:4; 2 Tim. 2:24).

4. *We must be convinced in our own minds that our conception of the goal and of the pattern is biblically sound.* For example, do we have a goal of interpersonal-interaction-in-small-groups merely because that is the fad in sociological circles, or is such interaction also a scriptural principle?

5. *We must help people to see the difference between the message, the basic ministry principles, the biblical goals for individuals, and current patterns and methods.* Many people will find it difficult to accept the idea that patterns and methods can change while the message, goals, and basic ministry principles remain constant. We must help them understand that maintaining a particular style of organization is not vitally important. On the other hand, maintaining the biblical goals for which the organization was originally brought into being *is* important. It may be well for us to remind folks that we are always guarding and maintaining the same basic truths that they hold dear. The only thing that we are suggesting they change is the style of organization, a current pattern, or a particular method. Also, we must try to make it clear that the reason we want to make such a change is to make the basics all the more effective in people's lives. We are not changing just for the sake of change, because change is never an end in itself.

6. *We must train people in goal-oriented thinking,* teaching them to ask frequently, "What is the purpose of this?"
7. *Many people will see the value of the goal, but since they cannot quickly figure out a promising means of reaching that goal, they may easily discard the goal.* We must remind them that if the goal is biblically sound, the Holy Spirit will, in time, lead them to find an appropriate means of reaching the goal.
8. *The single most crucial factor that determines the extent to which people will change is their motivation to change.* They must *want* to change. But in order to want to make a particular change, they *must become aware of the need* for it. By clearly seeing *both* the scriptural goals and principles as well as their present lack or weakness, they will see the need and, in turn, be motivated. Thus, two processes are necessary for motivation: first, a long educational process so that people can clearly visualize *what should be.* Second, a patient examination of *what is,* evaluated in light of what should be.
9. *We must keep in mind that change is much more probable when a person tells himself to change than when someone else tells him to change.* Therefore, we must lead him through a process of *self*-evaluation. Many self-evaluation guides are available, or we can devise one ourselves. Such a guide should be used only after the people can understand and appreciate the material in it. Their evaluations of themselves will be accurate and valuable only if they are as objective as possible. We must remember that people are more likely to be objective about themselves when (1) we are gentle (nonthreatening) with them, (2) we are objective about ourselves and are "human" in their eyes (admitting our own weaknesses and failures), and (3) we guide them through a long educational process which serves as a basis for their own self-evaluation.
10. *We must work with the pastors.* They are the key to change in the local church. Likewise, if we would like to see a change in the Sunday school, we must work with the Sunday school superintendent and the existing structure, staying within the channels.
11. *We must realize that whenever a church pattern or method is changed, people's attention will be drawn to the novelty of the change.* Therefore, they may be quick to say that the new approach is not accomplishing anything

simply because the newness of the approach has grabbed most of their attention. For example, suppose that a pastor wants to make a particular point in the middle of his sermon, so he asks several young people to pantomime a narrated scene. After the sermon, many folks, not being used to any such "shenanigans," would be able to remember what method was used. However, since they were distracted by the newness of the method, they may have missed the point of the narrated scene.

Typically, people will be quick to want to return to the old familiar ways of doing things and will feel that they are "getting more out of it," since their thoughts can now focus on the content being presented. Thus, we need to give people sufficient time to become accustomed to new methods and patterns. It may also help to warn them ahead of time that they will be distracted by the novelty of the new method, and that they should consciously focus their attention on the message.

12. *We must be sure that we are analyzing the present situation accurately.* We should beware of superficial judgments (John 7:24). A balanced perspective is important. All things considered, many evangelical and fundamental churches are doing a great deal right! We should frequently remind ourselves of that.

13. *We must beware of evaluations which are stated as generalizations.* (Examples: "The evangelical church today is not doing the job." "This program is not accomplishing anything.") Be specific.

14. *We must not tear down without also building up.* We must keep our criticisms constructive, have our goals clearly in mind, and focus our thoughts and comments to others on the positive goals rather than on the negative aspects of the present situation.

15. *We must beware of giving our evaluations before people are ready for them.* People are always quick to defend themselves. As much as possible, we must avoid threatening them personally by our evaluation. If they think that we think they have failed, they will probably have a strong drive to prove (both to themselves and to us) that they have not, making the prospect for change very unlikely.

16. *We must remember that the most significant area of change is within people, not programs or methods.* It is

all too easy to change the organization without changing the people.

17. *We must remember that inner change cannot be forced.* We should beware of too much change too soon. We should try to discover their pace, remembering that only a few will be eager for change. An idea once tried and rejected (because it was ill-timed) is unlikely to be tried again.

18. *We must work long and hard to gain the people's acceptance, then their approval, then their support.* We can easily have their acceptance without their approval, or their approval without their support. If we demonstrate a warm concern for the whole person, they will know that we are "on their side." Who wants to support someone whom he suspects is not on his side?

19. *We must strive for an objective understanding of the people's opinion of us and their view of our function in relation to them.* How do the people really think of us and our role?

20. *We must keep channels of communication open,* being sensitive to others' feeling about change and about us. We must build plenty of feedback into the new program, actively seeking feedback, not waiting for it to come spontaneously.

21. *We must be open and honest.* When we are defensive by covering up our real selves and are afraid to admit weaknesses or failures, others will respond with more of the same. Defensive people do not change. An individual may subconsciously feel, "If I do it *his* way, I have to admit that I was wrong. And since I do not like to admit error, I will not change and do it his way."

22. *We should deal personally with the stubborn person* so that he won't be so quick to judge our motives falsely.

23. *We must not seek a powerful office or position from which we can "decree" changes.* Without the understanding and support of the people, such changes will be short-lived; or, if "enforced" over a longer period of time, such changes cause ill will between us and others.

24. *We must provide concrete examples of how our ideas will "pan out."* People will want to see it work before they try it. We should visit a church that has successfully adopted some of our ideas, or ask people from such churches to

come and share and encourage our church members.

25. *We shouldn't try to adopt complete patterns or programs from another church.* What works in their church may flop in ours.

26. *We should avoid trial and error (thinking that if people try it they will like it).* If we have not guided them through an extended educational process, they will evaluate success or failure on the basis of their prior conceptions of the way things should be. They may still be looking merely for "numbers," smooth-running meetings, or good-sounding answers from students, and if our new patterns do not provide these things, they will feel that our new patterns are a failure.

27. *We must never argue about change.* Arguments only solidify people in their old thinking patterns.

28. *We must give all the people affected by a possible change a voice in discussing the reason for the change and the nature and direction of the change.* We should take the time necessary to arrive at a concensus rather than being satisfied with a mere majority vote. Several options should be examined together and either-or choices (such as, "either we adopt my new idea or we make no change at all") should be avoided. We must remain flexible and open to others' ideas if we want them to do the same.

29. *Often new labels (for groups or procedures) will help people think in new patterns.* Using scriptural labels might help the people remember that their new group or procedure is based on the Bible.

30. *We must be realistic,* making plans, not for ideal Christians, but for real-life, imperfect humans. Often an existing pattern of ministry, which deals with real, faltering humans, is compared with a proposed pattern in which ideal human participation is envisioned. Such comparisons are unfair, and such planning can be dangerous.

31. *When people envision themselves in unfamiliar roles, they feel uncomfortable—afraid of the unknown.* We should assure them of training and continued assistance in their new roles.

32. *We must determine in each instance whether gradual change or abrupt change is best.* Some situations call for very gradual, step-by-step change, in which the people are allowed to become accustomed to each new element

before introducing the next new element. Other situations are best changed all at once, so we shouldn't cut off a dog's tail a little at a time.

33. *We must avoid forming in-groups of progressive-thinking-renewal-oriented people,* which cause resentment and further resistance to change. Rather, we must identify ourselves with *all* the people and their basic goals. We must avoid the temptation to quickly withdraw and start new progressive churches.

34. *After we have accomplished all the desired changes (as if that were possible), we need to remain open and evaluate fairly the changes that the next generation will suggest.* If it seems difficult, we can see how the average church member feels about us!

CONCLUSION

Underneath it all is a simple choice. In attempting to effect change we can decide to be either a bulldozer or an educator. We must keep in mind that it is not just the scenery that needs to be changed, but *people.* A person who has been pushed around does one of two things. Either he pushes back, or he gets out of the way. Neither one of these reactions is desirable. We don't want to create resistance, nor do we want people to leave the church. Thus, we must be careful to function not as bulldozers, but as patient educators. *We, with our people (like the Holy Spirit with us), must be gentle teachers encouraging inner change on the part of our beloved brothers in Christ.*